THE
GREAT LAKES

Featuring the Photography of Julian Essam
CLB 1019
© 1985 Illustrations and text: Colour Library Books Ltd.,
    Guildford, Surrey, England.
Text filmsetting by Acesetters Ltd., Richmond, Surrey, England.
All rights reserved.
Published 1985 by Crescent Books, distributed by Crown Publishers, Inc.
Printed in Spain.
ISBN 0 517 440997
h g f e d c b a

THE GREAT LAKES

Text by

ANN Mc CARTHY

CRESCENT BOOKS
NEW YORK

The snow stayed, avalanching or blowing into broad, steep-walled, amphitheater-shaped valleys. Year after year it melted during the summer months and then refroze, making ice which blanketed the entire basin. The ice giant, born between one and two million years ago during the Pleistocene epoch, squeezed out of its cradle and crept down the valley.

The Glacial Period or Ice Age still exists in Antarctica and Greenland, but it ended in North America a few thousand years ago. The earth became bitterly cold during that period and four million square miles of moving ice buried most of North America. The gigantic mass, stretching from Hudson Bay to Long Island and the lower Ohio and Missouri Rivers, was over 10,000 feet thick near its center. Pushing through soil and rocks with powerful fingers, the continental glacier redirected the flow of rivers, gouged gorges, formed lakes and created waterfalls.

Four times the icecaps advanced, deepening existing basins and joining smaller ones. Finally, about 20,000 years ago, the Wisconsin glacier retreated and the land reappeared. The earth emerged with ancient valleys reshaped by glacial erosion, and edged with deposits, called moraines. The valleys filled with water, and the Great Lakes were formed. Centuries passed and, one by one, each of the "five sisters" made her debut. Together they would cover nearly 95,000 square miles of North America, making them the greatest expanse of fresh water on earth.

Lake Superior – 350 miles long, 160 miles wide and 1,333 feet deep at its maximum – is second largest in size only to the salty Caspian Sea. Erie, Michigan and Huron rank twelfth, sixth and fifth respectively. Even Lake Ontario places a respectable fourteenth among the world's largest lakes. Water drains from west to east through Lakes Superior, Michigan, Huron, Erie and Ontario, and eventually by way of the St. Lawrence River to the Atlantic Ocean. Between Lake Erie and Lake Ontario, the water plunges over 325 feet of limestone cliff with an explosive force, forming the most spectacular natural phenomenon on the Great Lakes shoreline: Niagara Falls.

The continental glacier forced Arctic animals to migrate south, as it destroyed vegetation along its path. When the ice sheets ebbed, the animals which had survived in warmer climates, and the trees and other plants, slowly returned to the freshly-scoured land.

Black and white spruce sprouted in the northern United States, followed by fir, larch and tall pine. Aspen, hemlock, and sugar maples with scarlet autumn leaves, grew later on the glacial valleys. The plains flaunted brilliant blooms of asters and goldenrod among the sedges and shrubs.

At the end of the Glacial Period, the Great Lakes area hosted a variety of animals. Because the larger animals needed more food and territory they had a slimmer chance for survival.

The gigantic mammoth, ancient ancestor of the elephant, was a towering fourteen feet with long, shaggy hair and eight-foot tusks. The mastodon – slightly less colossal – had short, coarse hair and small, upward-curving tusks. These behemoths roamed the Great Lakes region 6,000 years ago. At the same time, whales swam in Lake Huron.

The hairy musk ox did not meet his demise like the mammoth and mastodon. Instead, he traveled to the

Arctic's frozen tundra. His heavy, pointed horns curved down and out, and his shoulders appeared humped because of thick, brownish hair. When man arrived, the hoofed caribou or reindeer had followed the footsteps of the musk ox. They have large, hand-shaped antlers, and wide feet for easy travel across the snow.

Another Great Lakes survivor of the Ice Age, the bison, or buffalo, ranged in herds of over 60 million from the Pacific to the Atlantic and as far south as the Gulf of Mexico. The white-tailed deer, the black bear and the beaver – North America's largest rodent – are all Great Lakes old-timers. One native that has persisted, despite all changes, is the nocturnal raccoon. City folk, who may never glimpse a bear or a moose, will see one of the thirty-one species of this precocious masked bandit. Many other cousins of the weasel family still roam the Great Lakes region as well.

Almost all the cats have gone to the Canadian side. The powerful cougar, for one, covered even more territory than the buffalo. This handsome carnivore, capable of tremendous speed, can leap thirty feet while pursuing a deer. Though the wary lynx is almost never seen, his spotted cousin, the bobcat, is sighted on occasion.

While wildlife of the Great Lakes area stretches from the Gulf of the St. Lawrence to Lake Superior country, there are three places where aspects of its past, present and future can be studied. Bruce Peninsula is ideal for considering disappearing species. It is a narrow remnant of the Niagara escarpment separating Georgian Bay from Lake Huron. Mankind has felt unwelcome on its three-hundred-foot ridge of fossil-filled Niagara dolomite, allowing examples of ancient wildlife to survive.

Wildlife patterns are in the process of evolving on Isle Royale, a forty-five-mile-long island located fifteen miles from Ontario in Lake Superior. About six hundred moose and a small population of timber wolves live there. Their coexistence raises several questions: will the moose stamp out the wolf, or will the wolf propagate so rapidly that he takes over? Will the wolf starve and die out while the moose endures, or will he simply control the moose population?

Point Pelee, on Lake Erie, is another living laboratory of today's wildlife. There is no trace of the past, because wind and waves change its shape daily, but the present

is well represented. The sand pit, only ten feet above the water, is a sanctuary for many varieties of animal. Point Pelee's two-thousand-acre marsh is protected by Canada. Bird lovers are enamored of the Point because it is a terminus on major flyways. By late spring, over a hundred species will have made an appearance. Together, Point Pelee, Bruce Peninsula and Isle Royale can tell the Great Lakes wildlife story.

During the advances and retreats of the giant glaciers, man appeared in the Great Lakes area. He probably crossed the Bering Strait region, between the U.S.S.R. and Alaska, at least 15,000 years ago. Those Indians, perhaps lured by a herd of mammoth or a band of musk ox, moved toward an unrevealed world. Traveling through forests, they hunted and fished, gathering berries, roots and wild grains as the changing climate nudged them onward.

Centuries passed before Paleo-Indian families ranged over all of North and South America. Although they had straight black hair and dark eyes, their other physical features varied widely. They carried simple weapons and tools, but invented new methods for working stone and seizing prey as they acclimated to their surroundings. The world's first metallurgists, the Old Copper Indians dug thousands of pits along Michigan's Upper Peninsula as well as on Isle Royale in Lake Superior. Those early miners traced the veins of pure copper showing on surface rocks. They heated the rocks, immediately chilled them with water, then hammered them with boulders or pried with wood, until the copper broke off. Taken to camp, the metal was made into weapons, tools and ornaments, such as spear points, knives, fishhooks, harpoons, gouges, chisels, punches and needles. They formed axes or flat adzes for woodworking, attaching them to wood or antler-bone. Their ornaments were few, usually beads in tubed or round shapes, bracelets and pendants. They used the tools to shape canoes out of white or paper birch logs and to construct sapling-framed, round-topped homes with coverings of bark, skin or mats. About 1000 B.C., the Old Copper Indians migrated north and the Mound Builders moved into the Great Lakes area.

Early North American Indians built thriving towns in the East, raised mounds that rivaled Mexico's pyramids, and created a network of trade that extended from the Great Lakes to the Gulf Coast. From Indiana to West Virginia, hundreds of conical dirt humps dot the Ohio

Valley. The first Burial Mounds were formed for ritual functions by people of the Adena culture between 1000 and 300 B.C. Writhing across the countryside, Ohio's great Serpent Mound raises many questions about its cryptic creators who practiced a cult of the dead, constructing mounds mostly for burial.

By the second century B.C., a new culture – Hopewell – had appeared in the Ohio Valley. Deriving its art style, death cult and mound-building practices from the Adena, it amplified them into the cultural pinnacle of the Burial Mound Period. The Hopewell Indians' skeletons indicate that they were of medium height, long-headed, stocky, with oval faces and "slanting" eyes. The men wore breechcloths and the women wraparound skirts of hide: both wore moccasins. Men pulled their long, black hair back into a knot, leaving a forelock in front. Women parted their hair in the middle, drawing it back behind the ears.

The Hopewells brought agriculture and trade to the Great Lakes region. Their crops were chiefly corn, squash, sunflowers for seeds, and tobacco. They were also skilled craftsmen and makers of musical instruments. Flutes were carved from bone and bound together by bands of copper or silver, and rattles were sculpted from turtle shells. They created tobacco pipes in the shape of people and animals, as well as handsome pottery, polished stones, copper ornaments and necklaces from bears' teeth and river pearls. Their artistry was never equaled by another North American Indian tribe.

The Hopewell Indians developed an extensive trade network, affecting most of the Great Lakes area. Exchange routes laced the region, providing artisans with raw materials for the extravagant items that filled the mound tombs. Obsidian, chipped into ceremonial blades, has been traced to rock outcrops in Yellowstone National Park. Embossed breastplates, ear ornaments and ritual weapons were hammered from copper nuggets found near Lake Superior. Mica sheets from the southern Appalachians were cut into silhouettes of hands, bird claws, animals and headless men, and shells from the Gulf Coast were fashioned into adornments. Future cultures benefited from that influx of raw materials to the Hopewell burial cult; their exquisite handcrafted works of art have been found throughout the country. One of the most unusual and handsome objects discovered during the exploration of the Adena

Mound was a stone pipe carved in the form of a human figure. It is eight inches high and the body extends almost the entire length of the smoking chamber, tapering from an opening between the feet to the top of the head at the mouthpiece. Although the mysterious Effigy Mounds, shaped like animals and humans appeared later, no culture could fill the vacuum left by the Hopewell's decline after A.D. 500.

For the next twelve hundred years the Woodland Indians settled in the Great Lakes area, numbering 100,000 at the time of the white man's arrival. They were divided into peoples of many tribes and languages. Three large groups surrounded the Great Lakes – Algonquian, Iroquoian and Siouxian. The most powerful and best-organized were the Iroquois, who lived along the eastern shore of Lake Ontario were bitter enemies of the Algonquian peoples. Because the Indians had no written language, they used "wampums," uniquely designed and colored beaded belts, to carry messages. Their living quarters ranged from bark-covered wigwams to many-familied long houses. Within the tribes were clans, each of which had its individual "totem" – a supposedly blood-related animal. The Indians worked hard, but they also played. They invented "bagataway." Holding long sticks with a net at one end, they hurled a ball toward the opponent's goal. When the French arrived they named the game lacrosse. The Indians applied it as a test of skill and strength and to train young men for the hunt and for war.

Warriors raided camps to avenge injury or to take spoils and captives. Sometimes the attacker would notify his enemy by sending a sheaf of arrows or a wampum belt painted scarlet. To die in battle was honorable, but to carry home the slain foes' scalps as a trophy of victory was even better. Some tribes ate parts of the bodies of particularly prestigious murdered warriors.

The Iroquoian tribes – the Eries, Hurons and Tionontati – settled by Lakes Erie and Huron. Most of the Great Lakes area was inhabited by Algonquian Indians. Above Lake Superior were Ojibwa or Chipewa, one of the largest nations north of Mexico, numbering at least 25,000. The Kickapoo, Sac, Menomonee and Fox squatted on Lake Michigan's western shore near the Ottawas. The Ottawa, Ojibwa and Potawatomi who lived between Lakes Huron and Michigan, joined in a loose confederacy, calling themselves the Three Fires.

In Indiana were the Miami and, in Illinois, the Kaskaskia and Peoria tribes.

Europeans learned their way in the wilderness from those people. The Indian furnished his birch-bark canoe and guided the strangers on their explorations. The white men followed ancient Indian trails for trade routes and learned to survive on corn, succotash and hominy. Indian names like Minnesota, Wisconsin, Illinois, Michigan, Ohio, Huron, Erie and Chicago were absorbed into the white man's world. And the North American Indian's twenty thousand years or more of triumph over cold, hunger and even war, was over. An adversary from across the sea would take advantage of him in trade and war, seize his land and shatter his civilization.

Indians revered the land and saw no virtue in private acquisition. What mattered most to them was their relationship with each other and with the earth. But the white man came and permanently disrupted that symbiotic relationship with nature.

Étienne Brûlé had survived two frigid winters huddled in one of the French settlements. He kept warm in one of the huts which were clustered below the massive cliff of Quebec, at the edge of the St. Lawrence River. A large party of young men had sailed up the river from their native France with Samuel de Champlain in 1608. All but eight of them died during the first winter.

Étienne Brûlé wondered what he might find upstream, inside the mysterious continent, and he was intrigued by the almost naked Algonquians who wandered into Quebec each summer.

In 1610, when a party of Algonquians came down the St. Lawrence to trade their furs for French knives and weapons, Champlain made a proposal. He would take an Indian youth back to France if they would take one of his young men into the wilderness. The Algonquian chief agreed and Étienne Brûlé went with the Indians. In late summer, the cavalcade left Quebec. Brûlé helped paddle the canoe, past the northern shore where Montreal would stand one day, toward a new life.

For the next twenty-one years he lived among the Indians. He abandoned French clothing for an animal-skin loincloth and moccasins. In winter he wore leggings and a loose jacket of bearskin. He learned the Indians' dialects and slept on the bare ground in flea-infested huts of sticks and bark. Without a grimace, he satisfied his hunger by dipping into their communal dish of sagamite, a gooey concoction of crushed corn into which chunks of meat, fish and a leavening of bear fat had been stirred. On celebration days, when the Indians killed one of the dogs that came around their camps, he ate his share.

Though Brûlé never recorded his adventures on paper, we know, through the accounts of Champlain and others, that he was the first white man to see a Great Lake. Brûlé's Algonquian companions avoided the route up the St. Lawrence and through Lakes Ontario and Erie because that was Iroquoian territory and the two nations were deadly enemies. Because the French had met the Algonquian and their neighbors, the Hurons, first, they became their allies against the Iroquois. Consequently, they, too, followed the alternate course up the narrower Ottawa River, which came to be known as the "fur traders' highway."

Brûlé and his friends headed up the Ottawa, plunging into unruly water and occasionally pulling the canoes by ropes through the rapids. After passing the panoramic bluff where the city of Ottawa stands today, they carried their canoes over thirty-five portages to Lake Nipissing. From there they paddled down the French River to Georgian Bay, situated at the northeast corner of Lake Huron. This was the first Great Lake to be seen by a white man.

On another occasion, the dauntless Brûlé trekked through the forests of western New York in search of potential allies for the Hurons. Because he traveled on obscure trails to avoid the Iroquois, he almost starved. Gambling on their mercy, he entered an Iroquoian village. He lost his bet. They tortured him, pulling out his beard hair by hair, ripping off his fingernails and poking him with sizzling sticks. When one of them reached for the religious medal he wore around his neck Brûlé said, "Touch that and you will die. And so will your family." At that moment lightning flashed and thunder echoed across the valley. Terrified, the superstitious Indians shrank back from the seemingly-supernatural white man. In an effort to regain his favor, they indulged him with their most sumptuous foods before escorting him back to the Huron country.

Brûlé was killed by his Huron friends in 1632.

Apparently whiskey was involved; the article of trade which had the most leverage with the Indians, but which benefited them the least. Brûlé, who was born on a small farm near Paris, was still a young man when he died in the Canadian wilderness where he had helped bridge the gap between the two worlds. Behind him would come a trickle of explorers and missionaries and, finally, a flood of European settlers.

In 1634 Jean Nicolet, delegated by Champlain, set out in search of China via the New World's waterways. He traveled up the Ottawa River, through Lake Michigan and Green Bay to the Fox River, where he encountered the Winnebago Indians. Nicolet never came close to China, but he was at the farthest northwestern point of North America yet to be reached by a white man. Nicolet, wearing the brightly-colored silk damask robe given to him to impress the Chinese Emperor, stood in sharp contrast to the nearly naked or commonly dressed Indians.

Nicolet had failed to find the Northwest Passage, but he had crossed the Straits of Mackinac, eventually entering a land which would yield not gold, but furs. Beaver and other furry pelts were carried to Montreal and Quebec before being transported to eagerly awaiting Europeans.

A quarter of a century later, the people of Montreal welcomed the largest flotilla ever to return from the Green Bay area. Pierre Esprit Radisson and his brother-in-law, Médart Chouart, Sieur de Groseillers, led the 360-canoe fleet. Pierre Radisson had been captured by the Mohawks, the most violent of the Iroquoians, when he was only sixteen years old. He spent a year and a half as the adopted son of the chief before escaping to a Dutch trading post near today's Albany. As he searched for his missing brother-in-law, he eluded the deadly Iroquois who "approached like foxes, attacked like lions and disappeared like birds." Radisson joined Groseillers west of Lake Superior. There they made lasting peace with the Menominees, while claiming more territory for New France. They located supply routes that would lead to Hudson Bay, a potential spot for a trading post. But the governor at Quebec didn't like the idea. In fact, he had Groseillers temporarily imprisoned. The indignant partners took their plan to England's King Charles II. Thus began the Hudson Bay Company and Radisson's life-long exchange of affections between the French and the British.

Pierre Jacques Marquette's single-minded mission was to save souls. He spent time with the Indians near Lake Superior and built a log chapel at the Straits of Mackinac. Marquette, who followed the course forged by Nicolet thirty-nine years earlier, went deeper into the wilds of the New World. He and Louis Joliet drifted down the quiet Wisconsin River and met the Mississippi, regarded by the Menominee Indians as the mightiest and most dangerous of all rivers. Marquette didn't convert as many Indians to Christianity as he wanted, but the souls he won to his cause remained faithful. He died near today's Chicago in 1675 and two years later a band of converted Indians brought his remains to his small chapel on St. Ignace at the Straits of Mackinac.

On August 7, 1679, Robert Cavelier, Sieur de la Salle, set off in the first sailing ship to cross the Great Lakes. La Salle's sixty-foot boat, the *Griffin*, traveled down the Niagara River into Lake Erie and then to Lake Huron through the Straits of Mackinac and Lake Michigan, finally arriving at Green Bay. Though La Salle's route was similar to Marquette's, his aspirations were not. La Salle sought riches and glory and began with the fur trade.

A few months after its maiden voyage, La Salle sent the fur-laden vessel back to Niagara. The *Griffin* was never seen again.

La Salle's story was not as uneventful or short-lived as his boat's, but his fate was as tragic. After establishing forts on the St. Joseph and Illinois Rivers, conquering frozen waterways by making sledges for canoes, claiming the whole Mississippi for France, and nearly dying from exhaustion, inclement weather or lack of food, the intrepid explorer was assassinated by three of his own men.

Through La Salle's tenacious and far-sighted struggles, the Great Lakes were to stay under French rule for close to three-quarters of a century. Then, in one of history's most famous, if brief, battles, control of the lakes passed into the hands of the British. General James Wolfe's Redcoats climbed the cliffs at Quebec early one morning, surprising the French garrison under the command of General Louis Montcalm, from whom they easily won the day.

Mackinac City, the northernmost town on Michigan's

Lower Peninsula, links Lakes Michigan and Huron. In 1714, the French moved their fort and trading post there from nearby St. Ignace, where Marquette had built his chapel. For almost fifty years the French traded colored beads, brandy, knives, fish hooks and blankets for the Indians' mink, muskrat and beaver pelts at Fort Michilimackinac.

As a result of their victory at Quebec in 1760 the British claimed all of North America. The consequences filtered down to the Indians at Mackinac, who preferred the friendly ways of the French to the clumsy, stilted English manner. In 1763 the Indian leader Pontiac plotted an attack against Fort Detroit at St. Ignace and Fort Michilimackinac.

On a sultry day in June, the Chippewas and the Sauks, friendly rival tribes, gathered outside Fort Michilimackinac to play "bagataway." English soldiers and officers watched as the players swung their webbed sticks in the air. Suddenly the ball sailed past the goal post and over the wall into the fort. Two of the Indians, ostensibly rushing to retrieve the ball, grabbed Captain George Etherington and Lieutenant Leslyle. Then the squaws handed the warriors tomahawks and knives which had been hidden under their blankets.

Before the startled soldiers had time to reach for their guns, several were killed. The frenetic Indians seemed to be totally out of control as they dipped their hands in the victims' blood and smeared themselves with it. Yet they left the French alone.

Alexander Henry, a young English trader who lived at the fort, had not watched the game. He was inside the fort writing letters in preparation for a trip to Montreal. When he heard the screams he looked out his window and saw the slaughter. Desperate, Henry ran to the house of his neighbor, a Frenchman named Charles de Langlade. But his pleas for help fell on deaf ears. An Indian slave woman sympathized with Henry and showed him a staircase leading to an attic. Henry tiptoed across a floor of loosely laid planks and hid behind a pile of birch-bark buckets. Moments later he heard someone ask Langlade if he had seen an Englishman. Langlade said "No," but the Indians investigated anyway. They climbed the stairs and looked around the attic but didn't see Henry.

The following day, the frustrated Indians returned to Langlade's house. This time, Mrs. Langlade, who had inadvertently discovered Henry, disclosed his whereabouts. Henry overheard the discourse and, deciding to die bravely, stood to meet the Indians. One of them grabbed him, poked a knife at his chest, and then for no apparent reason said, "I won't kill you."

Henry was taken captive and a few days later, as he faced the Chippewa chief who was about to seal his fate, his long-time friend Chief Wawatam walked in. He carried goods which he offered in exchange for Henry's life. The warriors smoked their pipes in silence. Then the chief rose and said, "We accept your gifts; you may take him home with you." Twenty seven Englishmen were killed that day, but Alexander Henry went to Mackinac with Chief Wawatam.

Pontiac continued his assaults on Forts Detroit and Niagara, covering much of the territory around Lakes Erie and Ontario. Finally, in 1768, when peace was declared between France and England, Pontiac received orders to lift his siege. The Indian had no choice. The following August Colonel John Bradstreet greeted him with a force of twelve hundred men. Pontiac traveled to Fort Ontario, in Oswego New York, where he surrendered and swore allegiance to King George III. Other Indian chiefs followed his lead. England's battle with the French and the Indians was over, but before long an even more formidable foe would spring up – the new Americans.

The American Revolution and the birth of the new nation shifted the stage of history further south. But when the fighting ended, the British still held strong interests north of the Great Lakes and it was only a matter of time before the two countries would fight again. It was almost predictable, in fact, that the fighting would break out on the Great Lakes themselves.

It happened in 1812, as the leaves of the trees along the shores of Lake Erie were beginning to color the countryside with splashes of red, yellow and brown.

The conflict, an upshot of the Napoleonic Wars, was launched on the indented coastline of eastern Lake Erie, near Sackets Harbor. Shipowners of neutral America continued to supply the French. The English retaliated by stopping the ships, searching them for British deserters and confiscating cargo. American "warhawks" wouldn't stand for that. Besides they wanted to annex Canada and eradicate the British and Indian connection. So, on June 18, 1812, the United States declared war on England again. The initial attempt to conquer Canada failed. However, the tiny American navy performed remarkably well. With "wooden ships and iron men" Commanders Stephen Decatur, Isaac Hull and Oliver Perry "fought at close quarters between fast, square-rigged frigates with forty or fifty guns ..."

The international boundary between the United States and Canada had been established at the Treaty of Paris that ended the American Revolution in 1783. The imaginary line was drawn by cartographers down the middle of the four Great Lakes and through the bottleneck of lakes at Niagara, Detroit, Mackinac and Sault Ste. Marie. Lake Erie was critical because the Americans controlled its eastern end, at Niagara, and the British the western end, at Detroit. Young Oliver Hazard Perry was engaged to rid the lake of the "foreign" warships.

Perry arrived at the tiny port at Erie, Pennsylvania, ready to tackle his Herculean task. However, he didn't have a fleet. Ships couldn't navigate past Niagara Falls, so Perry waited patiently while his boats were being built.

Finally, at dawn on September 10, the nine ships of the American fleet were anchored in Lake Erie's Put-in-Bay, near Sandusky, Ohio. A lookout at the masthead shouted, "Sail ho!" Boatswains' pipes shrilled as the sailors scurried to their posts. Perry signalled from his flagship, the *Lawrence*, "Enemy in sight! Get under way!"

As the Americans sailed out of Put-in-Bay, the British fleet of six warships, under the command of Captain Robert Heriot Barclay, advanced toward them from the Detroit area. Perry had more ships, but the British had more experience of naval combat, their ships were larger and their cannons were accurate from a longer range. Perry needed to sail closer to his target, but the wind was against him. Then the wind shifted and his *Lawrence* was in range of the enemy's discharge. Cannonballs punctured its sides, as Perry unfurled a large blue flag with the valiant command, "Don't give up the ship!"

Cheers rose from the crew of the *Lawrence* and nearby ships as the flag was hoisted up to the foreroyal. Drums and fifes called the men to their battle stations and the captain bellowed, "All hands, all hands, all hands to quarters!" The gap between the British flagship *Detroit* and the *Lawrence* had closed to a mile. "Sail closer!" Perry commanded as shot pierced his vessel. Kentucky sharpshooters climbed the rigging. From the swaying towers they fired their rifles at British sailors with deadly accuracy. Unfortunately, the *Lawrence* was demolished and eighty three of the 103 men aboard were killed or wounded. Perry was forced to give up the ship but he wouldn't concede to losing the battle. He lowered the blue banner and, with the remnant of his crew, rowed to the approaching *Niagara*. The pennant which bore Perry's historic exhortation was raised and the *Niagara* headed toward the British fleet. When the Americans were almost on top of their targets, they fired, over and over again. The *Detroit* and the *Queen Charlotte* collided. Other brigs were destroyed, then finally, a British officer tied a white handkerchief to a boarding pike and waved it.

Formalities are inherent in naval warfare. Both victory and defeat are traditionally handled in a gentlemanly manner. Perry returned to the ravaged *Lawrence* and, in full dress uniform, accepted the surrender. He said, "Keep your swords, sirs, they have been bravely used and worn." Then he sent an American officer to the *Detroit* to express his respect for Barclay and his regret that he had been wounded. Next he wrote the renowned note: "We have met the enemy and they are ours...two ships, two brigs, one schooner, one sloop..."

Perry's gallantry toward the vanquished reached remarkable heights. When he discovered that payroll funds hadn't been delivered to the British base at Detroit, he lent his prisoners one thousand dollars. The result of Perry's congenial gestures was a lifelong friendship with Barclay.

Gunfire wasn't the Great Lakes ships' only antagonist. Through the centuries thousands of vessels have disappeared mysteriously, and others have been seemingly swallowed in the midst of a storm. The recently discovered *Scourge* and her sister ship, the *Hamilton*, met their demise on Lake Ontario 170 years ago. Those United States navy vessels were put into service during the War of 1812. The *Scourge*, an armed schooner, was originally a Canadian merchant vessel called *Lord Nelson*. The ship still bears the figurehead of the British naval hero Horatio Nelson.

In the early hours of August 8, 1813, *Hamilton* and *Scourge* were overtaken by a sudden, violent squall as they lay becalmed within sight of a British squadron in western Lake Ontario. Faltering under the lash of the gale, they swamped and almost instantly went down. Both ships were lost, carrying all but sixteen crew members with them. One of the survivors of the *Scourge*, Ned Myers, had traveled with James Fenimore Cooper on a merchant ship. In 1843, Myers contacted Cooper, who had become one of America's foremost writers. Recalling facts which had been locked in his memory for 30 years, Myers recounted his entire maritime story to Cooper, including the night the *Scourge* and *Hamilton* went down. The fusion of Myers' remarkable memory and Cooper's proficiency as a penman resulted in the classic naval drama, *Ned Myers; or A Life Before the Mast.*

The following excerpt from Cooper's book must echo the experiences of thousands of sailors who were trapped in maelstroms on the Great Lakes:

"We first spliced the mainbrace (had a ration of rum) and then got our suppers, eating between the guns, where we generally messed...As all hands were pretty well tired, we lay down, with our heads on shotboxes, and soon went to sleep.

"I ought to have said something of the state of our decks...There was a box of cannister, and another of grape, at each gun besides extra stands of both, under the shotracks...Each gun's crew slept at the gun and its opposite, thus dividing the people pretty equally on both sides of the deck. Those who were stationed below, slept below. I think it quite possible that, as the night grew cool...some of the men stole below to get warmer berths...

"I was soon asleep...How long my nap lasted, or what took place in the interval, I cannot say. I awoke, however, in consequence of large drops of rain falling on my face...When I opened my eyes, it was so dark I could not see the length of the deck...I now remember to have heard a strange rushing noise to windward as I went towards the forward hatch...One hand was on the bitts, and a foot was on the ladder, when a flash of lightning almost blinded me. The thunder came at the next instant, and with it a rushing of winds that fairly smothered the clap.

"The instant I was aware there was a squall, I sprang for the jibsheet. Being captain of the forecastle, I knew where to find it, and threw it loose at a jerk...The water was now up to my breast and I knew the schooner must go over...

"All this occupied less than a minute. The flashes of lightning were incessant, and nearly blinded me...The schooner was filled with shrieks and cries of the men to leeward, who were lying jammed under the guns, shotboxes, shot and other heavy things that had gone down as the vessel fell over...

"I succeeded in hauling myself up to windward...Here I met William Deer, the boatswain, and a black boy of the name of Philips, who was the powder boy of our gun. 'Deer, she's gone!' I said. The boatswain made no answer...

"I now crawled aft, on the upper side of the bulwarks, amid a most awful and infernal din of thunder, and shrieks, and dazzling flashes of lightning; the wind blowing all the while like a tornado. When I reached the port of my own gun, I put a foot in, thinking to step on the muzzle of the piece; but it had gone to leeward with all the rest, and I fell through the port, until I brought up with my arms.

"I struggled up again and continued working my way aft...I could not swim a stroke, and it crossed my mind to get one of the sweeps to keep me afloat...The water was pouring down the cabin companionway like a sluice; and as I stood for an instant...I saw Mr. Osgood (*Scourge's* captain), with his head and part of his shoulders through one of the cabin windows, struggling to get out...I saw him but a moment, by means of a flash of lightning, and I think he must have seen me. At the same time, there was a man visible on the end of the mainboom, holding on by the clew of his sail. I do not know who it was. This man probably saw me, and that I was about to spring; for he called out, 'Don't jump overboard! The schooner is righting.'

"I was not in a state of mind to reflect much on anything. I do not think more than three or four minutes, if as many, had passed since the squall struck us, and there I was standing on the vessel's quarter, led by Providence more than by any discretion of my own. It now came across me that if the schooner should right she was filled and must go down, and that she might carry me with her in the suction, I made a spring therefore and fell into the water several feet from the place where I had stood. It is my opinion the schooner sunk as I left her. I went down some distance myself, and when I came up to the surface, I began to swim vigorously for the first time in my life. I think I swam several yards...until I felt my hand hit something hard. I made another stroke, and felt my hand pass down the side of an object that I knew at once was a clinkerbuilt boat. I belonged to this boat, and I now recollected that she had been towing astern. Until that instant I had not thought of her, but thus was I led in the dark to the best possible means of saving my life...

"My first look was for the schooner. She had disappeared, and I supposed she was just settling under water. It rained as if the floodgates of heaven were opened, and it lightened awfully...

"I could hear many (men) around me, and, occasionally, I saw the heads of men, struggling in the lake...I now saw a man quite near the boat; and...made a spring amidships, catching this poor fellow by the collar. He was very near gone; and I had a great deal of difficulty in getting him in over the gunwhale...

"I now looked about me, and heard another...I caught him by the collar too; and had to drag him in...I kept calling out to encourage the swimmers...As the boat drifted along, she reached another man, whom I caught also by the collar...We had now as many in the boat as it would carry, and...it would not do to take in any more...

"The lake had swallowed up the rest...and the *Scourge*, as had been often predicted, had literally become a coffin to a large portion of her people."

Fortunately, more people have been transported over the Great Lakes than have been buried within them. The most massive human migration in history has been from Europe to the Western Great Lake States and Canada.

In the middle decades of the 19th century, European immigrants fleeing famine, oppression or war in their homelands, streamed into the fertile Great Lakes country. They harvested its forests, plowed its soil, mined its underground riches. Simultaneously, a network of transportation – steamboats, canals, railroads and turnpikes – developed to transport America's natural resources to industrial and commercial centers.

The Irish, prompted by potato crop failures, left their homeland for a better life in the New World. But the "better life" was slow to be realized.

The typical Irishman who landed at Halifax, Boston, and New York was met by a "runner" who bought the indenture paper, paid the vessel master, and found the immigrant a room in a run-down boarding house. Then the runner sold his investment to contractors who were building the Erie Canal across upper New York State. The Irish assimilated quickly. For the most part they kept moving westward – with the Erie Canal. A cholera outbreak in 1832 precipitated a shortage of men and a pay increase from $3 a month to $18. They dug the Erie Canal across New York, then the Wabash into Indiana and, finally, the Illinois canals. Now it was time for the trained work force to build railroads.

The canals and railbeds the Irish built would transport other nationalities into the Midwest. They would come in better style because of the Irish, but the Irishman had a head start in America.

The impetus for Scandanavian immigration is told through a character in Harlan Hatcher's book, *The Great Lakes*. Young Gustav Unonius was dissatisfied with the stratified society in Sweden and decided to go to America where "every workman has the same right of citizenship as the nobles." So, in 1840, he boarded a clipper at Gavle, Sweden and sailed for New York with his bride, her maid, a cousin and two friends. They were allowed the low fare of twenty six dollars per person if they brought their own bedding. Unonius obtained little information about the great West from New Yorkers, but a fellow Swede from Illinois told him that he must go there. That was good enough for Gustav. He and his friends went up the Hudson to Albany and across the Erie Canal to Buffalo. On the trip they met a man from Wisconsin who said that was the place to be. Crossing Lake Erie, they met a man who seconded that opinion. The six Swedes got off the boat at Milwaukee.

They settled at a spot thirty miles west at Pine Lake and wrote home to tell their friends about their wonderful new homeland. Other university students, former army officers and fallen nobles followed them, creating the first Swedish colony in Wisconsin. In the late 1840s nearly every craft arriving at the port of Milwaukee brought Norwegians and Swedes, causing the population to leap from 21,000 in 1850 to 46,000 in 1851. The American dream was real, especially around the Great Lakes. You could buy land for $1.50 an acre, a horse for $40.00 and a cow for $10.00. The government wasn't militaristic and religion could be practiced openly.

The Lake Superior Copper Mining Companies sent a representative to Sweden in 1864 to recruit ten thousand miners, offering to lend the ocean fare. The Swedes accepted contracts to mine copper for $250 a year. They also cut lumber in Wisconsin pineries, sailed ships on the Great Lakes and pushed wheelbarrows filled with wheat and iron ore. They put their money into farms which they chopped out of the Wisconsin forest. Over one fifth of the population of Norway and Sweden had come to America by 1900. A quarter million Swedes were in Minnesota; 200,000 in Illinois; 50,000 in Michigan and 48,000 in Wisconsin.

Germans had been steadily trickling into the Great Lakes region since the early 1800s, but the largest flow arrived in 1830 and 1848. Uprisings in Berlin, Vienna and Baden were activated by the unproductive Revolution of 1848. It began with a demonstration in Paris, but affected the 5,000 Germans who emigrated to America in the three years after 1848. Included in the gifted population of former revolutionary leaders and sympathizers were journalists, lawyers and teachers. Their destination was Wisconsin because of its inexpensive land. However, their intellectual talents were not in demand there so they turned to farming. Wagonloads of wheat and barley were hauled to Milwaukee for transshipment. Eventually Milwaukee became known for its high-skill machine tool builders. Michigan yearned for the German immigrants who became such skilled technicians, going so far as to publish a guide book in the German language. Though the Germans were first-rate machinists, musicians and farmers, they have received the greatest acclaim for their beermaking.

While Irish, Scandanavians and Germans arrived in especially large waves, many other nations also relinquished their adventurous or their oppressed. Occasionally an entire Swiss village would emigrate, thus relieving congestion at home. The Dutch came for timbering, settling mostly in Michigan. When the timber was gone, they bought the chiseled land and planted tulips and celery. Polish people put down stakes in Cleveland, Flint, Buffalo and other Great Lakes towns. When the pine was consumed, they moved into mining. The Danes became Great Lakes dairymen; the Finns mined the Marquette Iron Range in the Upper Michigan Peninsula, before moving west to the Menomoniee, Gogebic, Vermilion and Mesabi. The Welsh mined; the Slavs and Romanians made steel; the Scots preferred the marine trade. The Canadians as well as the Americans welcomed the Europeans with open arms. It would take an inexhaustible number of people to fill their Great Lakes land.

America's first settlers viewed the land very differently from the white man. Sioux Chief Luther Standing Bear poignantly expressed the feelings of his people: "We did not think of the great open plains, the beautiful rolling hills, and winding streams with tangled growth, as 'wild'. Only to the white man was nature a 'wilderness' and only to him was the land 'infested' with 'wild' animals and 'savage' people. To us it was tame. Earth was bountiful and we were surrounded with the blessings of the Great Mystery. Not until the hairy man from the East came and with brutal frenzy heaped injustices on us and the families we loved was it 'wild' for us. When the very animals of the forest began fleeing from his approach, then it was that for us the 'Wild West' began."

Though Tecumseh and other Indian chiefs restated their belief that it isn't right for individuals to own land, millions of acres of bountyland warrants were issued to veterans of the American Revolution. They read:

"To all whom these presents shall come greetings: Know ye that in consideration of Military Services performed, as a member of the Continental Establishment in the Great Rebellion, there is granted to said veteran in lieu of monies: 100 acres in the United States Bounty Lands.
G. Washington"

That land included territory north and west of the Ohio River, but the veteran wasn't entitled to go into the territory and simply measure his own hundred acres. He had to wait until the government surveyed and partitioned it, and that took time. They were often forced to sell their warrants at a substantial discount price to land jobbers who later redeemed them at full face value. So they took their chances by responding to advertisements in Eastern journals:

"One million acres of Ohio Country now open to sale and settlement. Equal to any part of the Federal Territory in point of quality of soil and excellent of climate. Veterans' bountyland warrants accepted at one third."

The advertisement guaranteed that horses, cattle and hogs could find abundant fodder, and that cotton, as well as all grains and vegetables would burgeon. However, the indebted farmer had four short years to produce the flourishing crops and complete his land payments. So he quickly built a makeshift cabin, and then handled the laborious task of clearing the land. After the trees were cleared and burned, the farmer chopped through a root mass with an ax. He planted in those holes, working around the logs which lay helterskelter. The first crop was understandably sparse – just enough to feed his family. Though the soil wouldn't be seasoned until his son's generation, he eventually produced enough to begin meeting his payments.

The settlers' first commercial crops were usually corn, then wheat. When they were unable to sell the grain in nearby cities, they used it to feed livestock. So, pork and beef became another source of income. The woods generated a small cash crop, too. Eastern pharmacists coveted the aromatic root of the ginseng plant which could be shipped economically. In 1815 wood ashes worth $120 per ton were sold for the manufacture of soap, glass and bleached cloth. But it was difficult to come up with a ton of ashes. Selling furs was another means of earning cash. However he managed it, when the farmer finally met his last payment it was time for a more permanent life style.

His wife had probably long ago chosen a spot for their new home. The cabin would have a puncheon floor and square timbers, joined by notch and dowel; and it would be clean and smell of maple. The farmer's plow didn't long survive its persistent abuse through woody roots. The worn hoe blades or horseshoes were nailed onto a curved mold board, carved from hardwood. The handles were of crooked white ash roots. The Southerner, up from Virginia, let the land guide his plow, while the Puritan Yankee strived for straight rows. In either case, the farmer's most enduring helpers were his sons, his ox and his horse. The original cabin often became a stable for the draft animals.

As soon as he could afford them, the farmer bought hogs for food and for marketing. Hogs multiplied twenty times faster than cattle and could walk a hundred miles to market without excessive weight loss. The farmer's sheep supplied the material to keep his family warm. Salt, needed for the animals as well as for curing and preserving food, was difficult to find.

The pioneer woman worked hard, and probably began her life near the Great Lakes in a dirtfloor hut, but she had pleasurable pursuits. She particularly enjoyed her kitchen garden. Potatoes, turnips, cabbages, parsnips and melons were planted in the center of the enclosure. Vining plants, like squash, cucumbers, beans and hops - were planted on the west fence. There was always a small bed of herbs, anise, basil, catnip, horehound, horseradish, mint, wintergreen, witch hazel and tansy. On the border were raspberry, currant and gooseberry bushes.

The farmer's persistence paid off. After twenty years, he had probably expanded his main house, cleared as much as seventy acres, built a large barn, and successfully marketed his grain. The pioneer's offspring and ensuing generations were the real beneficiaries of his tenacity. Today, throughout the Great Lakes country, crops flourish in the fertile soil. And along the highways, and behind them, are reminders of the pioneer woman's affection for flowers. She carried orange day lilies and pink scrub roses in boxes and pots, before transplanting them in the alien earth.

It was a treat for the pioneers to add fruit to their meat and potato diet. And there really was a John Chapman, better known as Johnny Appleseed. He especially loved apple trees. In 1800 Chapman left his farm orchard outside Pittsburgh and headed northwest. He carried a bag of appleseeds, a bag of meal, a lump of salt, a Bible, a hatchet, hoe, rake, flint and steel. By planting apple seeds in pioneer settlements, he was "making the wilderness fruitful." Chapman gathered his seeds at cider presses and distributed them in the spring, teaching the settlers how to propagate and care for apple trees. Chapman befriended the Indians who mistook him for a medicine man. He planted herbs along with his trees to make teas and poultices to soothe wounds and burns.

Though not totally appreciated in his day, future

generations reaped the benefits of his determination. In Michigan he left seeds with missionary priests instructing them to mulch and wrap the trunks in winter. And his nurseries near Fort Wayne, Indiana, have yielded fifteen thousand trees.

Though none attained Chapman's fame, other Great Lakes residents grew apple trees. Several Canadian settlers had orchards. One of them, John McIntosh of Dundas County, transplanted a number of wild apple trees in 1796. He nurtured them until he had a perfect specimen. He named it McIntosh Red, and it has become one of the world's best eating apples.

When Sieur de la Mothe Cadillac founded Detroit in 1701, he brought a gardener with him from Quebec. Giant pear trees were the main attraction in his orchard. Examples of these impressive trees survive in Monroe and Waterworks Park, Detroit. Of an original group of twelve representing the apostles, only Judas stands today. For years Michigan led the orchard-growing states, but the planting which began at Aurora in 1805 turned Western New York into impressive orchard country.

The farmer conquered the problem of inadequate soil, but was unable to transport his produce to a major marketing center until the early 1830s, when the Erie Canal began operating. With the development of the canal system, the Western states became a part of the commercial world. By 1836, steel rails invaded the land, and schooners and side-wheelers plied the Great Lakes, making routes to Eastern markets accessible.

In 1839 Ohio, New York and Pennsylvania produced more than half the total wheat crop grown on the American continent. Twenty years later they relinquished their lead to Illinois, Indiana and Wisconsin. The completion of the Soo Canal at Sault Ste. Marie allowed Minnesota and the Plains States to join the Great Lakes traffic. Today, a half million bushels of wheat, harvested from twenty thousand acres in Minnesota, can be carried on a single vessel.

Wisconsin discovered its specialty in 1870 - dairy farming. The state became the world leader in dairying and the five hundred people from Glarus, Switzerland, who had been sent to New Glarus, developed their own cheese. Their Swiss process for making it became widely popular. Today, Wisconsin produces half the cheese made in the United States and exports large quantities to Europe.

Throughout the Great Lakes countryside, families are managing the farms of their ancestors. Usually there are several structures behind the main house which were built to accommodate needs through the decades. And often way in the rear is the original cabin. The complex is a reminder of our forefathers' courage and perseverance.

At one time a pristine forest stretched north of the Great Lakes two thousand miles from Nova Scotia to Lake of the Woods, and south to Western Ohio. But lumber became big business, and trees fell like dominoes. In record-breaking time the woods were plundered and parts of the Great Lakes region were completely devoid of pine. Great Lakes steamers and clippers assisted the lumber operation. Seven hundred vessels carried the wood across the Lakes in 1885. Another deluge of logs went down the Mississippi.

Sawmills sprang up in hundreds of lake and river towns. Sixty large sawmills rose above the twin industry capitals, Bay City and Saginaw, Michigan, in 1880.

Lumber camps became lumber towns. Snarling saws, smells of chipped wood, and entire towns constructed of unpainted wood were their trademarks. The roads were logs, the sidewalks duckboards, the houses squared timbers. The ground along the Huron shore was covered with sawdust and shavings. Eight hundred logging camps and twenty five thousand loggers invaded the Michigan woods. In spring, French Canadians came out of Mackinac's woods to spend a winter's pay in one of Saginaw's thirty two saloons. Timber came into Detroit, Toledo, Cleveland, Buffalo and Toronto, as the swelling nation used 350 cubic feet of lumber for each man, woman and child every year. Because of thinning forests, the lumbering frontier moved west. Eighty five millionaires, and sailing fleets that could haul a billion board feet a year, emerged from Muskegon's lumber kingdom. The town, on Lake Michigan's east coast, flaunted first-rate saloons, gambling houses, and red-lighted hotels. Most of Muskegon's lumber built Chicago and nearby prairie cities. Chicago was a wooden town before Mrs. O'Leary's cow knocked over a bucket, starting the blaze which brought down the city in 1871. The saws moved on to Wisconsin and Minnesota, finally reaching Duluth, the Great Lakes' westernmost city.

The frontiersmen had harvested the forests; now it was time to excavate the land. Mining ore began in Pittsburgh, then in Ohio, where Daniel Heaton introduced the furnace as a means of refining ore. However, the output of seven tons of iron required an acre of trees for charcoal. Before long, a more advanced process for refining minerals was developed and, with the help of a magnetic compass needle, an ore with a larger quantity of iron was discovered in Michigan. The Marquette Iron Range was especially rich with minerals. Michigan's success stories intrigued Cleveland men. Samuel L. Mather, a young lawyer descended from the Cotton Mather family of New England, thought that the ore couldn't be successfully smelted in Michigan. He suggested that the ore be taken to Cleveland, just as the coal from southern Ohio and Kentucky was transported there via the Ohio River and Lake Erie. The resulting iron would be a short distance from its market and the Midwest would have a giant, three way commerce.

The Cleveland Iron Mining Company was formed with Mather as its secretary. The company sent a group of men up to the Marquette Iron Range to chop ore out of Cleveland Mountain. In spite of the bitterly cold winter and a land claim dispute with the Marquette Company, the miners hacked out a thousand tons of ore. It was taken by sled eighteen miles to Lake Superior, and when the ice melted, it was floated in barrels to Sault Ste. Marie at St. Mary's River. There, passage to Lake Huron was obstructed. Mules hauled the barrels around the rapids, then they were floated to Cleveland. After all that, the going price was only $8 a ton.

Mathers remained enthusiastic, and encouraged his miners to keep digging. However, something had to be done about the portage situation at Sault Ste. Marie. The cargo was unloaded and portaged through town and around the rapids by horsedrawn cars. At times, an entire vessel was towed over the land. A canal at the Soo was clearly needed, but the Federal Government refused to finance the project.

Then, in 1852, Charles Harvey, a twenty four-year-old scale salesman for the Fairbanks Company of Vermont, came upon the scene. As he sold scales to merchants and miners he looked for moneymaking opportunities. Unfortunately, the first thing he acquired at the Soo was a case of typhoid. While recuperating, he watched the ships being towed through St. Mary's main street. He wrote to the Fairbanks Company urging them to undertake the building of the canal: "A three quarter mile canal here not costing over $400,000 would enable any craft to load at Buffalo and go through to Fond du Lac 600 miles west of here..." he explained. Land grants were available, and Harvey was sure the canal would make them a fortune. By 1853 Charles Harvey had imported a thousand men to build a canal that would ultimately cost $1,000,000. They had mechanical difficulties and faulty materials, and Harvey turned out to be a better salesman than engineer. Nevertheless, the canal's tandem locks, each carrying a vessel up or down nine feet, began operating on June 18, 1855. The *Illinois*, a wooden steamer, made the first passage up from Lake Huron to Lake Superior.

In August 1855, the brig *Columbia* locked down the Soo carrying 132 bulk tons of Marquette ore. The brig was bound for the Cuyahoga River in Cleveland, where the ore would be consigned to Hewitt and Tuttle for resale. Most of the 7,000 tons which came to Cleveland the next year were sold by Hewitt and Tuttle. Business was booming so they hired another clerk. His name was John D. Rockefeller. Tuttle started out by giving the bright sixteen year old a bit of advice: "Don't ever again accept a job without asking what your wages will be." They agreed on $3.50 a week.

Two years later Rockefeller was promoted to bookkeeper, receiving $500 a year. Before long he asked for $800 a year, but the firm offered $700. In 1859 he resigned, borrowed $1,000 from his father at 10 percent interest, found a partner and hung up a sign: Clarke & Rockefeller – Grain, Hay, Meat – miscellaneous.

Rockefeller's experience with iron ore and iron shipping would come into play later, but his real game would eventually be petroleum.

Meanwhile the miners continued to blast with gunpowder, shattering rocks which the men crushed with hammers. As the broken rock was brought up, the shafts grew deeper. The miners who were lifted and lowered in "cages" supported by cables, carried picks, axes, harness, lanterns and shovels. A candle in their hat provided the only illumination in the dark shafts. The ore was raised in buckets. However, by the end of the 1900s, those mining methods would become obsolete. Engines, electric motors and lights, mechanical crushers and dynamite modernized the operations.

In time bigger and better mine fields were discovered, including the Menominee Range and the Gogebic, which put Hurley, Wisconsin on the map. Though Ironwood, Michigan developed as the business capital of the new range, Hurley, with 58 saloons, 20 hotels, two dry goods stores and a minister, became the favorite local spot for nightlife.

In the 1880s, when the great railroad building era came to an end, some feared that the demand for iron would terminate too. However, Maj. William Le Baron Jenney appeased those concerns by coming up with a revolutionary use for steel. He convinced Chicago architects to replace thick building walls with strong steel frames and lighter coverings. Those sturdy buildings could reach unprecedented heights, and that would take a lot of steel. Additionally, an Illinois farmer discovered that twisted steel wire, made into fencing, would keep the cattle away from his corn. Barbed wire became important when John W. "BetaMillion" Gates, an opportunist and super salesman, sold barbed wire from Illinois to Minnesota and then to the Plains States. The quantities he sold built scores of wire mills around the Great Lakes. Over a twenty seven-year period, Gates united all the major wire producers into the huge American Steel and Wire Company, becoming one of the nation's wealthiest men. His next vision was to merge the entire steel industry. So he approached J.P. Morgan, America's foremost financier. Morgan didn't like Gates, but he liked his idea. Before long, Morgan owned Gates' companies and Gates added a half billion dollars to his bank account. That transaction created the Federal Steel Company.

The clamor for steel nails and steel tubing for bicycles prompted businessmen to search for even richer ore. The Vermilion Range and the Soudan Mine near Duluth put Minnesota in the iron business. The deposits were discovered by the Merritt brothers who were in the area surveying lumber. Their father had told them, "When you're looking up at timber, look down also at the ground." In 1890, the four brothers and three cousins were camped on stony hills which the Indians had named "Mesabi" (height of land). There, under the nine-inch-thick layer of pine needles, was red dirt. It was not hard like other iron ore, but powdery. They rushed to Duluth to have it tested. It was 64 percent iron!

The Merritt brothers were on easy street. They had found what they believed to be a lifelong source of wealth. They sold the land they had acquired over the years and put the cash into buying and leasing the fortune-producing hills. However, the former timber-seekers, who were soon mortgaged beyond restoration, didn't impress investors. They had at their hands more ore than anyone had ever owned, but no means to mine it. They traveled to Pittsburgh to see the world's most celebrated steel man, Andrew Carnegie. But that was a dead-end street. Carnegie didn't like dealing with ore. Then the brothers discovered an even larger quarry, Mesabi Mountain, but their railroad construction was deepening their debt $10,000 a day.

While minerals were being mined John D. Rockefeller created the Standard Oil Company in Cleveland. Anxious businessmen told him that the Merritts' plight could become the nation's crisis. Rockefeller wasn't interested in ore, but trusted advisers informed him of the Mesabi's superior deposits. Besides, by bailing out the Merritt brothers he would assure the completion of railroads and prevent financial ruin for thousands of businessmen. Rockefeller would think about it.

He didn't succumb to pressure until Frederick T. Gates, a man he respected, wired him of impending disaster: "Must have some money at once (if you want to) save Merritt boys' collateral, which means control of the best properties. Complete collapse of Merritt-Wetmore syndicate, and Merritts personally and Duluth, Mesabi, and Northern R.R. now mere question of days." So, Rockefeller, the oil king, went into the iron ore business. The steel giants – Carnegie, Morgan, Frick and Gates – knew that Rockefeller did nothing in a small way. Would their new competitor build a steel mill? Would his prices be lower than theirs? They had good reason to be nervous.

The Mesabi was rapidly outshipping all other ranges combined. On top of that, Rockefeller had learned from his crude oil experiences to control his own transportation. So he created another advantage in his clash for power with the steelmakers. The son of Samuel L. Mather, Samuel Mather, of Pickands Mather Company, was highly regarded. Rockefeller asked him to orchestrate the construction of his ships. Mather declined. He wasn't interested in providing transportation for his competitor. Rockefeller reasoned that since he was going to build anyway shouldn't

Mather have the commission. Mather wasn't interested until Rockefeller presented his next argument.

"Of course, Mr. Mather, but I had in mind twentyfour (ships)." Twenty four! That was different. Sam Mather realized that he had better be in charge of the operation. An order that size could unbalance the lakes and tie up all the yards, raising the cost of ships for everyone else. The order eventually diminished to twelve, but it was still sizable. Mather went about wheeling and dealing with wisdom. He contacted several shipyards, sending each a set of plans and specifications for "one or two ships if bids are attractive enough at this time."

Each shipbuilder was invited to Mather's office on a specific Wednesday to discuss his bid. One by one, the builders walked out of Mather's office smiling smugly at the other contestants. Each was certain he had the winning bid.

Rockefeller called his twelve, new, 475-foot-long ships the Bessemer Fleet, and added existing vessels to it. The ships carried Carnegie's ore. Carnegie's partner, Henry W. Oliver, and his chief operating officer, Henry Clay Frick, cautioned him about the contract. It made him too dependent on Rockefeller. But the Scotsman reiterated: "Ore will prove to be the least profitable and most troublesome aspect of the steel business." Then he sent an ultimatum to Rockefeller to cut his carrying rates in half, adding, "Better accept."

Rockefeller headquarters in New York replied by transmitting messages to all Bessemer agents and captains. In a short time, throughout the Great Lakes, boats transporting Carnegie ore lost their way and smoke was seen rising from the stacks of anchored boats. Carnegie's mills were an endangered species. The expedient Scotsman paid the full rate.

The next contenders to enter the ring were the tycoons, Rockefeller and J.P. Morgan. Judge Elbert H. Gary, Morgan's right-hand man, made it clear to Morgan that U.S. Steel must acquire Rockefeller's Mesabi ore and the Bessemer Fleet. But Morgan had a problem. The way to accomplish the acquisition was for him to talk with Rockefeller. "I don't like the man. I would not even think of it." Morgan, however, realizing the size of the stakes, came to his senses. He sent an ambassador to invite Rockefeller to come to his office at Number One Wall Street. Rockefeller refused.

The irate banker roared. That was it. He had done his part. A few weeks passed before Morgan was pacified and tried again. This time Rockefeller sent his son, John D. Jr., not yet thirty. He sat in the banking magnate's office for several minutes without being acknowledged. Morgan was absorbed in conversation with his partner, Charles Steele. Finally, Morgan looked at young Rockefeller, "Well...what's your price?" he bellowed.

Rockefeller retained his composure, "Mr. Morgan, I think there must be some mistake. I did not come to sell. I understood you wished to buy." The Rockefeller Mesabi was incorporated into U.S. Steel for $80 million in stock, and control of the Bessemer Fleet for $8.5 million. Rockefeller was off the water, but his fleet was put into the Pittsburgh Steamship Company. The entire operation became known as the Steel Trust Fleet.

In the future that fleet and others would have access to all the Great Lakes. Though no longer deterred by narrow passageways, the ships would continue to be harassed by turbulent storms and cruel weather.

The Great Lakes play an important role as weather-makers. The large bodies of water retain their temperatures and seem to wield a soothing influence on the air that passes over them. When spring comes to the Midwest, tornados come with it. But the lakeside cities seldom see them. Fall weather is an inheritance from summer. After storing up summer's heat, the Great Lakes give it back to the atmosphere in the fall. The air, gradually becoming colder than the water, takes its heat from the water. As this transference occurs, it tempers the chill, extending the growing season on the shore.

However, the Lakes also host tempestuous storms. Winds from the west and south gather moisture, then cool and drop their moisture as snow or rain on the leeward side of the Lakes. As much as seven inches of rain may suddenly be deposited on Gary, Indiana or lower and upper Michigan across Lake Superior; in the winter it's a blitz of snow. Erie has a different problem. Its abrupt high rise of land forces the moisture-laden air currents rapidly upward. These surprise attacks are precipitated by a collision of water temperature and land temperature. Open water temperature does not go below 32 degrees. One unheralded storm dropped five feet of snow on Oswega, New York, in 1972 causing meteorologists, who were gathered at a national meeting, to be marooned for three days.

Despite impulsive storms, the Great Lakes have lured masses of people to their shores for 150 years. Today, a seventh of all United States citizens and a fourth of all Canadians congregate in the area. The lower Great Lakes and Southern Lake Michigan are feeling the pressure caused by that cloudburst of people. Cities, farms and industries pollute the rivers that flow into them.

Before the mid-1950s most monitoring efforts centered on navigational problems, water-level control and fisheries of the nearly 5,500 cubic miles of Great Lakes water. To analyze the water's contents seemed impossible – there was so much of it. But something had to be done. Scientists began to analyze water samples and, over the years, they saw an increase in dissolved solids, including the nutrients phosphorus and nitrogen. During a 60-year period only in Lake Superior was no ascertainable increase found. Lake Huron had experienced a 10 percent increase; Lake Michigan, 20 percent and both Erie and Ontario had increases of more than 30 percent.

Canada and the United States share four of the Great Lakes and eight border the U.S. shoreline. The Federal Departments of Agriculture, Commerce, Interior, and Transportation each have some responsibility for the Lakes, but the Environmental Protection Agency has primary control of cleanup. Each Lake has its own characteristics. Even the water flows through them at a different rate. Lake Superior is the largest body of fresh water in the world. Its volume equals that of all the other Great Lakes combined, plus three more Lake Eries. The depth at its maximum is 1,290 feet. Rugged, high bluffs, unspoiled forests and expansive sand beaches surround the clear, cold water. It is the "shining big sea water" of Longfellow's *Hiawatha*.

But to the French it was "supérieur." The wilderness disappears at the lake's far western corner, where Duluth-Superior and Thunder Bay load ocean-going freighters with grain and ore. About 45 million tons of cargo pass through the ports at Duluth, Minnesota, and Superior, Wisconsin. Foreign flags and names of faraway ports lettered on the sterns of "salties" add a feeling of romance to the harbors. Most of the ships that tie up at the world's largest ore-loading dock are long, black-hulled "lakers," however. Almost as long as three football fields, the newest lakers can hold 50,000 tons or more.

Above Duluth an area called Split Rock extends from Split Rock Lighthouse to Gooseberry State Park. The name "split rock" came from two high cliffs just east of the Split Rock River's mouth. Viewed from a certain position on Lake Superior, the rocks appear to be split apart. The well-known beacon, Split Rock Lighthouse, sits on the point. The lighthouse, an important aid to mariners from 1910 to 1968, was equipped with a 370,000 candle power light. When it was no longer used to warn ships of this dangerous part of the North Shore, it became a landmark.

Isle Royale, a U.S. National Park and wilderness preserve, is Lake Superior's largest island. There are lodges on the 45-mile-long island, but its primary appeal is to campers, hikers and wilderness lovers.

Lake Superior's shores are lined with wild beauty. Along the southern shore, Wisconsin's Apostle Islands and Michigan's Pictured Rocks have been named National Lakeshore areas. Grand Portage, Minnesota, on the west, has been designated a National Monument, and Canada has established Sibley Provincial Park on the western shore and Lake Superior Provincial Park on the east. Michigan adds her share to the landscape with the ruggedly-beautiful Keewenaw Peninsula.

Superior feeds the other lakes by emptying into the St. Mary's River at the Twin Cities of Sault Ste. Marie in Michigan and Ontario. The famed Soo Canals there, with four locks on the U.S. side and one on the Canadian, carry twice the traffic of the Panama Canal. The largest lock, 1,200 feet by 110 feet, can handle even the largest laker.

At the end of St. Mary's River is Lake Huron. In size and cleanliness it ranks second to Lake Superior. Georgian Bay, its longest arm, lies in Canada and is separated from Lake Huron's main body by the Saugeen Peninsula and Manitoulin Island. Eighty-mile-long Manitoulin is the world's largest island in a freshwater lake. In the Ojibwa tongue it's the "holy place." Tourists seem to agree with that label. Though farming is the main industry, tourism is a steadily growing second. Outsiders savor its picturesque scenery, quiet villages and hundreds of tranquil lakes. Huron's only sizable cities are Sarnia, Ontario, with a population of 60,000 and Bay City, Michigan, at Saginaw Bay, where the U.S. border indents. There are two groups of Georgian Bay Islands

National Park in Canada, one near Midland, and the other at the tip of the slender Bruce Peninsula near Tobermory.

Mackinac Island stands guard at the Western entrance to Lake Huron. Perched on its green bluffs is the Grand Hotel, a massive white building encircled by an intricately-carved veranda. Below is often heard the clip-clop of a horse and buggy because all motor vehicles are banned. In the summer, yachts fill the harbor and the population swells as visitors enjoy the 19th-century atmosphere. In the winter the population shrinks to 500 year-round residents.

St. Ignace sits on the southernmost part of Michigan's Upper Peninsula, and Mackinac City is located on the northern tip of Michigan's Lower Peninsula. In 1957 a bridge was built at the junction of Lakes Michigan and Huron to link the two pieces of land. Mackinac Bridge, affectionately called Mighty Mac, stretches for five miles across the Straits of Mackinac. Each year, on Labor Day, thousands participate in a promenade across the bridge, leaving just a narrow path for cars.

Boats travel between Lakes Huron and Michigan beneath the bridge. Lake Michigan, the fifth largest body of fresh water, is the only Great Lake totally within the United States. Michigan has a split personality. Much of its northern shore is virgin territory, but its southern end supports an intensive concentration of people and industry. Chicago epitomizes that phenomenon. From its shores, the band of development continues eastward around the Calumet district of Indiana and northward to Milwaukee.

The Indians gave Milwaukee its name (meeting place of the rivers), but the Germans gave the city its flavor. They arrived by boat in the early 19th century, bringing their love of good music, good brew and their recipes for schnitzel and spaetzle with them. The transplanted culture translated into a 13,000-acre park system, a fine symphony orchestra, an opera company, good restaurants and world-renowned breweries.

Milwaukee is often called "the machine shop of the world" because 40 percent of its work force is employed on assembly lines. In its 2400 factories, Milwaukee turns out such products as sausages, electronics, leather, and fine graphics. Milwaukee steam shovels helped gouge the Panama Canal; the city's turbine engines were used in retraining Niagara Falls, and its gears have operated rolling mills all the way to Japan.

Lake Michigan has a critical role in the distribution of these manufactured goods. The natural harbor at Milwaukee, often compared to the Bay of Naples, provides an exit to the world's markets. Ferry boats bound for Michigan visit Milwaukee's busy harbor which is crowded with pleasure boats of all kinds.

Though Milwaukee excels in production, people are its greatest resource. In the mid 19th century, the enlightened intellectual Forty-Eighters left Germany, fleeing political revolutions and bringing with them new educational and social ideas that made an immense contribution to the city's cultural and political life. Carl Schurz, later Secretary of the Interior, was one of their leaders, as was Eric Seidel, the first Socialist Mayor of an American city (Seidel's secretary was a young man named Carl Sandburg). Other famous Milwaukeans have included General Douglas MacArthur; James Peck of Bad Boy fame; movie stars Spencer Tracy and Pat O'Brien, and Golda Meir.

Where the suburbs of the Wisconsin city end, a utopia for vacationers begins. Green Bay, on the Wisconsin shore, has the Door Peninsula, and on the east the two Traverse Bays, Great and Little, are studded with resorts. Nearby is the Sleeping Bear Dunes National Lakeshore, a 400-foot-high desert on Lake Michigan.

If Wisconsin is shaped like a mitten, then Door County is the thumb. Or, if Wisconsin is shaped like a teakettle, then Door County is the spout. From any viewpoint, Door County is a long, narrow peninsula that juts out into Lake Michigan with a rugged 250-mile shoreline that has earned it a reputation as the Cape Cod of the Midwest. Its steep limestone cliffs plunge to sandy beaches and forests of pine.

Off the point of the peninsula is Washington Island, which can only be reached by a 40-minute ferry ride from Gill's Rock. The ferry goes through a narrow strait once called Death's Door, for the hundreds of ships that fell prey to its perilous currents in the late 1800s. Museums on the island display Potawatomi Indian artifacts and curiosities that once belonged to early settlers. Nearby Jackson Harbor flaunts old fishing shacks and dunes and swailes at its Natural Area.

Door County is famous for shipbuilding, antiques, specialty shops, a thriving dairy industry, parks and cherry and apple orchards, which are just as popular to visit during blossom time as during fall harvest. You can pick your own fruit at several of the cherry, apple and pear orchards. A Door County tradition is the fish boil. Trout or white fish are boiled in washtubs with onions and potatoes. When the chowder is just done, oil is tossed into the pot, generating great bubbles and a swirl of fire.

Ephraim is called the Summer Capital of Door County. A church steeple stands at each end of its crescent-shaped harbor. The charming village was settled by Moravians from Norway, and their no-liquor stricture still holds. The ancient Norwegian midsummer celebrations are still going strong, too, and thousands of tourists join in the festivities.

The Ridges Sanctuary near Baileys Harbor is made up of 700 acres of beach ridges covered with spruce and tamarack. More than 25 species of orchids live in its arboreal forests. Sturgeon Bay is a major Great Lakes shipbuilding area, and cherries are made into wine at the von Stiehl Winery in Algoma.

On the other side of Lake Michigan, and farther south, sits Chicago, a great American megalopolis. Unlike cities that cover their waterfronts with wharves and industry, Chicago cherishes its lake. Lake Michigan is Chicago's prairie to the east; its source of pleasure and peace. Four hundred and thirty sprawling parks fringe most of the magnificent, 29-mile lakefront. In the summer sunbathers swarm to the 31 beaches and hundreds of boats line the harbors.

Behind the expanse of blue and carpet of green, stately buildings and skyscrapers mark the beginning of an aggressive, brawny city. The backdrop of buildings cushions the clamor of heavy traffic and congested neighborhoods. Though many of the city's characteristics are found in other towns, in Chicago they are exaggerated. Chicago has the "biggests," the "bests," the "firsts" and the "foremosts." It is a city of bravado and that bravado is translated into optimism, tenacity and courage. Some of Chicago's firsts are Sara Lee cakes, the *Encyclopaedia Britannica*, the *World Book*, McCormick's reaper, Pullman's railroad cars, the zipper, the lie detector, cafeterias and mail-order catalogues from firms like Sears, Montgomery Ward

and Speigel. Chicago is also famous for Schwinn bicycles, Zenith TV, Motorola radios, Wrigley's gum, Quaker Oats, International Harvester and McDonald's hamburgers.

Chicago is reputed to have its first for infamy too. Characters like Al Capone and his cohorts, and Big Jim Colosimo are a part of the city's history. But then every big city has its seamy side. It's just that in Chicago even the gangsters are larger than life.

A couple of Chicago's best are novelist Saul Bellow, who won the Nobel Prize for Literature, and The University of Chicago's economist Milton Friedman, who received the Nobel Prize in Economics.

Though New York's population more than doubles Chicago's 7,500,000 within the city, no one can deny that Chicago has the biggest or, rather, tallest buildings. The Sears Tower, the world's loftiest, soars above the Loop. At 1,454 feet and 110 stories, it is more than a hundred feet higher than New York's twin-towered World Trade Center and more than two hundred feet higher than the once-preeminent Empire State Building. Chicago's white marble Standard Oil Building, called "Big Stan," is the world's fourth tallest building. And soaring above the Near North Side's "Magnificent Mile" shopping mecca is the 100-storey John Hancock Center, or "Big John," fifth tallest in the world. It is a self-contained complex of condominiums, offices, stores, restaurants and garages. A 92nd-floor condominium owner claims to live in the world's highest apartment.

The Gold Coast, along Michigan's lakefront, was once home for the Potter Palmers, the Swifts, the Montgomery Wards, the Armours, the McCormicks and the Kimballs. Most of the elegant mansions have been replaced by luxury high-rise condominiums for those who haven't fled to the suburbs.

Chicago is "a city that had to be" because it occupies the point where the prairie, Lake Michigan and the Chicago River converge. At the close of the last Ice Age, debris from the glacier-gouged lakebed rose about six feet from the surrounding prairie flatness, creating a watershed which divides the Mississippi and the Great Lakes-St. Lawrence water systems. French-Canadians Father Jacques Marquette and Louis Joliet portaged at that spot in 1673. A canal made passage by water a reality in 1848, thus creating an inland water link between the North Atlantic and the Gulf of Mexico.

The canal connected the headwaters of the Chicago River, a part of the Great Lakes system, with the Des Plaines River, a part of the Mississippi system. Prompted by the canal builders in the 1840s, then by the railroad builders in the 1850s, the small frontier village became the country's transportation and distribution hub within a few decades.

Whether by air, rail or water, Chicago maintains that historic role as the nation's transportation center. O'Hare International, handling 44 million passengers a year, is the world's busiest airport. And mile after mile of freight cars still line the tracks of Chicago's Cicero switching yard. The terminal, with a capacity of 3,000 cars, does a turn-over business. The average length of stay for the freight cars is only 15.5 hours. A third of the nation's capital goods are shipped from this area, which dominates Pittsburgh in steel production and outranks West Germany's Ruhr Valley in industrial output. Just one of the steelmaking plants in the Calumet Region, Inland Steel's Indiana Harbor Works in East Chicago, has 23,000 employees. The industrial colossus was responsible for some of the dirtiest air and water along Lake Michigan's shoreline. That was over ten years ago, before the Federal Government got into the pollution control business.

Now you can see the bottom through twenty feet of water on most days and the State has restocked the lake with salmon and trout. Fishermen who go after the chinook and coho salmon on the Chicago Transit Authority's rental boats, catch "CTA Salmon" and lots of it! The greasy ring on the sides of ships is gone. The skies are cleaned up too, but they aren't perfect. Through the haze of Lake Michigan's horizon emerges the hulk of a freighter carrying Minnesota ore, Michigan limestone and Scotch whisky, imported through the St. Lawrence Seaway. She is headed for the Port of Chicago, headquarters of the enormous steel-producing, oil refining industrial complex, stretching from the city's Far South Side to Hammond and Gary, Indiana and further.

Gary, third largest city in Indiana, was an industrial miracle of the twentieth century. In 1906, Judge Elbert Gary, then Chairman of U.S. Steel Corporation, came up with the idea to build the largest integrated steel mill in the world. To accomplish that task, 12,000 acres of dunes were leveled, $100 million was spent, and within a decade, Gary, 53 square miles in area, housed, serviced and employed more people than any other town of its size. Gary is on the southwest tip of Lake Michigan's curve and the Indiana Dunes are on the southeast.

The Indiana Dunes National Lakeshore Park is a magnificent 12,000 acres of sun-flecked woods, marsh, bog, lagoons, high dunes and 20 miles of beach. Though the dunes are not as tall as those at Sleeping Bear and other Michigan locations, they stretch miles farther inland. Their base is sand rather than glacial till. The northwesterly wind and currents bring sand down the Lake from communities as far north as Waukegan, Illinois, and sweep it into this southernmost point on the shore. All dune areas follow a pattern of natural succession from the newly-formed beach, back to the foredune, then the pine forest, and finally to the oldest area, the climax forest.

The accumulated swell of Lakes Michigan and Huron empty into the St. Clair River at the cities of Sarnia and Port Huron and then into Lake St. Clair. The Canadian shoreline of the 460-square-mile lake is mostly undeveloped and Walpole Island in the center is occupied by an Indian Reservation. The contrast at the southwestern end is sharp. Windsor is on the Canadian side and across the strait, the suburbs of Detroit sprawl for miles. At Belle Island, Lake St. Clark meets the Detroit River, the busiest inland waterway in the world. At that point Lake Erie enters the scene.

Lake Erie is the oldest, shallowest, busiest and dirtiest of the Great Lakes. And it's a sailor's nightmare. When storms come out of the west, the saucer-shaped lake becomes a treacherous body of water. One of these squalls can cause a thirteen-foot difference in water level at opposite ends of the Lake.

Erie's western basin is shallow, with depths of 30 feet or less. However, the bottom stairsteps down into the 80-foot-deep central basin, and finally into the eastern basin, whose deepest point is 210 feet. It's not surprising that Lake Erie is heavily polluted. Eighty percent of its water flows from Lake Huron, past heavily industrialized Detroit. Much of the rest comes from streams that flow out of business centers like Cleveland's Cuyahoga River. Erie's bottom is coated with a sediment layer that ranges from 30 to 125 feet thick. Normally sediment traps excess phosphate, but when the water's oxygen is depleted by dying algae, the iron compound breaks down again, releasing the phosphate and stimulating further growth.

Algae feed on nutrients from sewage plants, industry and agricultural runoff. Phosphorus and nitrogen are nutrients and phosphorus can be easily removed from incoming wastes. Furthermore, Lake Erie has a faster natural flushing rate than any of the other Great Lakes. So, if the deluge of contaminants is slowed, perhaps they can eventually be swept downstream and into the Atlantic Ocean.

Paradoxically, two of the Great Lakes' most troublesome culprits came up from the Atlantic. One is the alewife, a seemingly innocuous member of the herring family. The other was the villainous sea-lamprey, an eel-like parasite as much as two feet long, with a suction mouth and barbed teeth. The lamprey entered Lake Erie by way of the Welland Canal in the 1920s. It rode piggy-back on a fellow fish or hitched itself to the hull of a ship. The less maneuverable alewife struggled upstream, finally arriving years later. Once through the canal, the lamprey moved all the way to Lake Superior, almost wiping out the trout.

In 1958 the U.S. and Canada began to fight back. A lampricide was developed which would kill the lamprey larvae without harming desirable fish. The result was a fast drop of about 80 percent of Lake Superior's lamprey population. Since then, the lamprey count has leveled off to between 10 and 20 percent of the original peak.

The mild-mannered alewife presented a different problem. After making its way through the Welland Canal in the 1930s, it simply devoured its rivals. The alewives would have fallen prey to lake trout and turbot, but the sea lampreys took care of them. The alewives ate up the zooplankton upon which other small fish lived, and soon themselves represented about half the fish population of the Great Lakes. Recently sharp changes in water temperature or, perhaps, the poisonous properties of algae, have caused the alewife population to lessen. Lakeshore residents hope that the lake trout and large numbers of coho and chinook salmon which have been successfully introduced into the Great Lakes will survive, and that the alewife will form a large part of their diet.

Today lakeside residents have a more immediate problem, however. All of the Lakes except Superior have suffered from high water, bringing wave damage and shore erosion. Portions of towns like Port Clinton, Ohio, on Lake Erie's southwestern shore, have been awash. A northeast storm there can last for ten days, and incoming waves can be as much as ten feet high. A ranting storm will take its toll on Erie's Bass Islands too.

Each summer more than a quarter of a million people visit South Bass, Lake Erie's most popular island. Middle Bass, Kelleys, North Bass and South Bass Islands are inhabited all year round. During the summer months hourly ferryboats carry 300 people a day to the bristling public islands. There are seven smaller islands as well. Private seasonal homes are established at Ballast, Rattlesnake and Sugar. The State of Ohio owns Gibraltar. Green, Starve and Mouse are uninhabited.

The eleven islands huddle around a granite pillar that rises 352 feet above the village of Put-in-Bay on South Bass Island. This Doric obelisk, erected in 1915, commemorates Commodore Oliver Hazard Perry's defeat of the British squadron in these waters during the War of 1812.

The islands boast of their bygone days. More than a century old, a clapboard hotel and circular bar still stand on Put-in-Bay's main street. Once the summer haunts of the rich and the famous, the Bass Islands have hosted Presidents and tycoons as well as bootleggers and gamblers. South Bass was once the home of the 825-room Hotel Victory. It took 350 craftsmen more than three years to build the huge wooden structure. In 1892 the Victory made its debut with ballrooms, gardens, and trolley cars that ran the two miles to the village. And then, on August 14, 1919 the Victory Hotel burned to the ground.

Unfortunately, that incident was the harbinger of things to come. The island's small wine industry almost met its demise because of Prohibition. The turn-of-the-century resorts became relics. The sturgeon and sauger were fished out. And Lake Erie began to strangle on the mainland's waste.

On top of that, the islanders' mascot and means of winter transportation fell into disrepair. Since 1935, the red-white-and-blue Island Airlines' Ford Tri-Motor, known as the Tin Goose, has bailed out the land-bound when Lake Erie froze over. Its short take-off and landing capabilities, oversize balloon tires, and tail-dragging landing gear made it perfect for island hopping. On July 1, 1977 the Tin Goose crashed on Bass Lake Island. A "Save the Goose" fund was begun and natives rallied to the cause. The Ford Tri-Motor was no ordinary airplane. It would be rebuilt.

The Victorian homes on Lake Erie's islands are surrounded by vineyards. The plump Catawba is king of the winegrower's grapes. Louis Heineman, the owner of Heineman Vineyards, is cellar master, chief field hand, salesman and caretaker. South Bass winemakers have seen better days. By 1880 more than 600 of the island's 1,300 acres were growing grapes to furnish 12 wineries and five brandy distilleries. The largest winery, the Put-in-Bay Wine Company, produced more than 150,000 gallons a year. Then Prohibition and the Depression impeded the burgeoning family operation.

Today only the Duff and Heineman vineyards are still in production and Heineman's present annual output is less than 30,000 gallons. Meier's Wine Cellars, however, does a large volume of business on North Bass.

North Bass is a 700-acre company island a half mile south of the Canadian border. Meier's Wine Cellars, Isle of St. George Vineyards, is the catalyst for 35 residents, 400 acres of grapes and two mechanical grape pickers. These are the largest continuous Catawba vineyards in the world. Because the climate is the same as the Rhine Valley, where the best Reisling grapes are grown, North Bass produces an excellent Reisling. Cold winters and cool summer nights are the necessary ingredients. Meier's ship 60 tons of grapes a day to the mainland winery.

Bigger isn't necessarily better, if you ask the residents of Middle Bass. They venerate the wines and champagnes of Leslie Bretz, who personally oversees his tiny winery. He regularly checks gauges, hoses and pumps in his old wooden, pressing barn which puts out 10,000 gallons a year.

Like the wine-makers, Lake Erie's fishermen have seen better times. Past generations caught 5,100 pounds of whitefish and 6,200 pounds of perch on a good day and boasted 300 commercial fishing boats and three fish buyers. Now there is only one commercial fishing boat working out of the islands.

Lake Erie was once the world's largest supplier of freshwater fish, but pollution and overfishing have greatly diminished production. In the past few years, fishing has begun to improve, largely because the Ohio

government has put a ban on commercial gill-netting. Waters surrounding the eleven islands are critical breeding grounds. Still industrial waste, urban sewage, and farmland runoff have added more life nutrients and microorganisms to the Lake than it can handle. Recent pollution monitoring and collection of ecological data have only stabilized conditions. Despite its troubles, Lake Erie continues to furnish more fish for the nation's consumption than the rest of the Great Lakes combined.

Above-water sailors make their mark in the Inter-Lake Regatta, one of the top-notch races in U.S. yachting. As many as 500 boats compete, coming from as far away as Argentina. And during the summer season Lake Erie's beaches are crowded with tourists.

Winter brings a different story and different sports. One of the most relaxing, if taxing, is ice-fishing. The lake is quiet and the ride across the frozen surface, between clusters of ice-fishing shanties, is peaceful. The canvas-covered fishing houses are installed in January when the lake ice thickens to about two feet. Inside, a stool, a small coal stove and a Thermos bottle are the meager accoutrements. In the spring a doorless convertible hauls the miniature house away.

Ice-sailing is another form of recreation on Lake Erie. It's fast and fun, but there are hazards. The sailboats can only run on snowless ice and that usually means early or late in the season when the ice is most fragile. If the boat takes a nose dive into the thin, mushy ice, then the escape for passengers is precarious. However, that doesn't discourage the hardy sailors, who are often the same ones who are on the open water in summer.

As the days become longer and warmer, islanders begin to prepare for the season's invasion of tourists. The outsiders disrupt the tranquility of the locals, but boost their economy and bring a form of excitement.

Detroit, Lake Erie's biggest city, has always had notoriety, but an event in the late 1890s introduced a name which has become synonymous with the town.

The night shift engineer for the Detroit Edison Company was bewildered. In his excitement to build a machine he called a quadricycle in the shed behind his house he neglected to build an exit. He didn't even know if the newfangled thing would work. He tore down part of the shed wall, rolled his motor car out to Bagley Street, and got in to start it up. Much to the surprise of the inventor, Henry Ford, "the darned thing ran."

That was June, 1896, five years short of Detroit's 200th birthday. The city was old by American standards, founded as a fort by the French before anyone had settled New Orleans or St. Louis. Though lumber barons were important to the town, it didn't have much national economic influence. By the turn of the century its population of 280,000 was about the same as Milwaukee's.

The Strait of Detroit (the city's name means "The Strait" in French) controls access between the upper and lower Great Lakes. In 1701, Sieur de la Mothe Cadillac was sent from Montreal to fortify the place. However, it wasn't until the completion of the Erie Canal that Detroit's growth began. It eventually became the transshipment point for the East and the newly-developed farmlands of fertile southern Michigan. Later in the century, resources from the north country funneled into the city. It was at that point Henry Ford and his friends entered the scene.

Henry Ford did not invent the assembly line. The technique, traced back as far as 18th-century England, was a common occurrence in American packing houses after the war. Ford was not even the first man to make cars. In 1899 Ransom E. Olds had gathered the capital to open a plant for commercial auto manufacture. And before that, Charles Brady King chugged down Detroit's streets in his four-cylinder, twenty-mile-per-hour gasoline car. But Ford was the first to apply the assembly line to the car industry.

Ford raised the money and hired Albert Kahn to build a factory in Highland Park. Seven years later, in 1913, 250,000 cars were turned out in the 260,000-square-foot plant and company profits came to $25 million. One man who put up $2,500 worth of stock sold it sixteen years later for more than $30 million. Competitors were incredulous. And there was more. In 1914 Ford announced the eight-hour, $5-dollar day, almost double the prevailing pay scale. Ford was dissatisfied with his Highland Park plant, however, so he bought 2,000 acres of land near the mouth of the Rouge River, southwest of Detroit. In 1920 the company transferred its entire operation to the new River Rouge plant, the largest in the country.

The Model T Ford is seen only on occasion now, usually when antique car collectors flaunt it in local parades. But the "Tin Lizzie" was owned by millions of Americans in its heyday. They cranked it by hand, shifted gears by foot, and removed the front seat to fill the gas tank. Proud owners bounced on its hard, narrow, bicycle-type tires along bumpy dirt roads. If any of them followed one of those roads south along Lake Erie, they would probably have found their way to Cleveland, Ohio.

Cleveland didn't just happen, like so many cities. Following the Revolutionary War, forty-nine Connecticut men purchased three million acres of land in far-off Ohio. One of their group, Moses Cleaveland, led a surveying party there in 1796 to establish a town where the Cuyahoga River spiraled into Lake Erie. Cleaveland unloaded his surveying instruments and laid out the city which straddled the Cuyahoga, then went back to his home in Connecticut. Cleaveland never returned to the city he named himself, and that may explain why they spelled his name wrong. The "a" vanished forever.

Cleveland was a small town until after the Civil War, when it became a key industrial center. Men like Mark Hanna and Samuel L. Mather reaped their fortunes from the burgeoning iron industry, and John D. Rockefeller founded the Standard Oil Company there. In time, such wealth was transformed into a public asset in the form of museums, theatres and concert halls. Cleveland, the eighth largest city in the United States, can take pride in its cultural and industrial legacy. Iron ore is brought to its shores from Lake Superior and coal is transshipped to other Great Lakes ports. However, the Cuyahoga River is in a sad state today. It is so heavily polluted with oil and chemicals that it is "the only river in the world to be proclaimed a fire hazard." It did catch fire in 1969, causing $100,000 worth of damage to two bridges. The claim of exclusivity isn't accurate, however. The Buffalo River, at the eastern end of Lake Erie, has been in flames several times.

East of Cleveland, Erie sits on the only piece of Pennsylvania that touches Lake Erie. And Pennsylvania had to struggle for that one port. The French built Fort Presque Isle at Erie in 1753, then the British took it and later the Indian Chief Pontiac burned it. But Erie survived, becoming a great U.S. shipyard. The fleet that cleared the British from Lake Erie under Commodore Perry was built there.

Erie is situated on a tiny triangle jutting out of Pennsylvania's roughly rectangular borders. Called the "Keystone State," Pennsylvania formed the cornerstone of the 13 others. William Penn deserves the credit for shaping the destiny of a land that Henry Adams described as the "ideal American state, easy, tolerant and contented."

When Penn and 100 followers set sail for the New World in September 1682, George Fox had a "bon voyage" message for them: "My friends that are...going over to make outward plantations in America, keep your own plantations in your hearts with the spirit and power of God, that your own vines and lilies be not hurt." Penn did exactly that.

The area between Erie and Buffalo is some of the most scenic on Lake Erie's shore. Had it not been for the most momentous engineering feat in the history of the young American republic, Oswego, instead of Buffalo, would have been New York's second largest city. When the Erie Canal opened for business, joining the Great Lakes to the economic mainstream, Buffalo was transformed from an obscure village to a booming port city. But though Buffalo was transformed, it didn't really come into its own until after the depression of 1837. Grain elevators rearranged its skyline, and only Chicago had larger stockyards. Its port competed with Cleveland's for the commercial traffic of the eastern Great Lakes. Even so, Buffalo is probably best remembered for hosting the Pan-American Exposition of 1901, the place where President McKinley was assassinated.

One way to get from Lake Erie to Lake Ontario is over Niagara Falls. Another more practical and pleasant means of passage is through the 27-mile-long Welland Canal. There, more than 100,000 cubic feet of water a second roars through tunnels to generate electricity for two nations and another 100,000 cubic feet per second plummets over a 193-foot cliff. Below the falls the deep Niagara River runs fast for seven miles before peacefully emerging into the last Great Lake. Lake Ontario is the smallest of the Great Lakes, covering only 7,550 square miles, though it is still larger than the state of New Jersey. Ontario is the second deepest lake, however, with a sounding of 283 feet. That depth has a nurturing effect on the surrounding countryside. One of the great fruit belts of North America surrounds its littoral. But deep water doesn't help Lake Ontario's

pollution problems which are second only to Erie's. They are partly inherited and partly the result of big cities' chemicals and algae-spawning discharge from sewage plants. Hamilton and Toronto on the Canadian side and Rochester and Oswego, New York, on the U.S. shore, contribute the major share of pollutants.

Rochester began as a mill on the Genesee River operated by an unsavory character named Ebenezer Allen. A loyalist during the Revolution, Allen was a self-confessed murderer and polygamist. He arrived in the Genesee Valley in 1782 and about six years later was given a 100-acre tract to operate a sawmill and gristmill at the Genesee Falls, in what is now the center of downtown Rochester. But his stay was short-lived. In 1791 Allen moved to upper Canada, never to be seen again. In 1811 Nathaniel Rochester came from Maryland and gave the city his name.

However, Allen's mills prospered and the Erie Canal made markets accessible. Rochester became known as the "Flour City." Then, in 1888 George Eastman brought his Brownie camera to Rochester, changing the face of the city forever.

The development of the camera and celluloid film made Eastman an extremely wealthy man. By the time of his death in 1932 he had given away $72 million, mostly to his hometown and the University of Rochester.

Ontario is the only Canadian province to span the Great Lakes. The nation's water-pollution research is concentrated at the Canada Centre for Inland Waters, at Burlington. There, scientists probe the physical, chemical, geological and biological processes occurring in the water. Canada and the United States are working through their International Joint Commission to save the Great Lakes, so valuable to both nations. They are beginning to take the essential steps of upgrading sewage treatment and enforcing pollution regulations.

Ontario, located in central Canada, is bordered by the James and Hudson Bays to the north, and by the St. Lawrence River and the Great Lakes to the south. One thousand miles across, Ontario touches New York on the southeast and Minnesota on the southwest. Exceeded only by Quebec in size, Ontario has a larger population than any other Province. Ontario meets the land where a third of the people of the United States live. Its industrial and agricultural maturation make Ontario Canada's greatest money-producing Province. The prosperous dominion is committed to a unity in a country which is divided by English and French sentiments. The official crest of Ontario is a shield with the Cross of St. George at the top and three maple leaves below. Over the shield is a bear, and at either side is a deer and a moose. Below is a Latin motto which translates: "Loyal she began, loyal she remains."

The Province is divided by a narrow neck of land between Georgian Bay and the Ottawa River. Southern, or Old Ontario is separated by the Niagara River. Americans can enter Ontario by crossing a bridge into the Canadian city of Niagara Falls.

The accumulated waters from the four western lakes found a new course from Lake Erie to Lake Ontario. Pouring over a sheer limestone precipice, the rushing water landed with an explosion. When the French explorer Father Louis Hennepin first saw the watery escarpment he was awe-struck: "This waterfall is 600 feet high," he later reported to his superiors. Niagara Falls is actually about 160 feet high, but Hennepin can be forgiven his lack of accuracy. Thousands of equally enthusiastic spectators have succeeded him, swarming to watch the water spill to a thunderous splashdown. Reportedly, Napoleon's brother brought his bride to the Falls by stagecoach from New Orleans about 1804. Though that particular story may be more fiction than fact, it is certainly true that grooms have been taking brides there for at least one hundred years. Along with its unprecedented attraction for honeymooners, its attraction for daredevil types has become legendary.

The first death-defying individual, Jean Francois Blondin, announced that he would walk across Niagara Falls on a tightrope hundreds of feet above the churning whirlpool. Crowds covered both shores when, on June 30, 1859, Blondin stepped on the cable and began his almost quarter-of-a-mile journey from the American to the Canadian side of the Falls. To balance himself he carried a thirty-eight-foot-long pole which weighed forty-five pounds. When he was about a hundred feet from the ledge, he sat down. Then he stretched out on his back, balancing the pole above him. Next he stood on one foot. Halfway across, he produced another crowd-pleaser. He dropped a rope to a steamboat, pulled up a bottle of champagne, drank from it, and completed his extraordinary feat.

Blondin wasn't content with the accomplishment of one audacious feat, or perhaps the accolades went to his head. In any case, on a subsequent trip across the wire he pushed a wheelbarrow with only a train's light for illumination; a third time he wore a blindfold and, for his finale, he carried a passenger on his back. Blondin and his trusting cargo almost met their demise. The rope sagged and a supporting guy wire broke, causing Blondin to poise on one foot. The two men finally made it; the onlookers roared. But, after that Blondin pursued more timid activities. In the future, several brave souls would tumble over the Falls in barrels, but Blondin had already reached the pinnacle of Niagara Falls theatrics.

Another way to approach Ontario is through Ottawa, the nation's capital. For a hundred years after Victoria chose Ottawa as the capital city, it sat stolidly on an Ontario bluff, looking down into French-Canadian Quebec. Governmental posts were held by English-speaking Canadians, who had little awareness of the French or their language. For the most part French-speaking people were consigned to clerical and menial jobs, provided they would speak English.

Today, thousands of Francophones occupy prestigious positions. The French language is not only acceptable, it is in vogue, and in demand at cocktail parties, dinners, plays and operas. Because of a billion-dollar bilingual and bicultural revolution, begun by Prime Minister Lester Pearson and continued under French-Canadian Prime Minister Trudeau, Ottawa has two official languages.

Simultaneous with the cultural improvements, Ottawa had a face lift. The Old World Parliament buildings and monuments are surrounded by miles of contemporary government office buildings. And French and English Canadians happily enjoy the dozens of parks which have bicycle and walking paths and are landscaped with millions of flowers. Everyone can choose from an assortment of intriguing restaurants, innovative theatre and fine concerts. An appreciative citizen, who may be a little chauvinistic, claims that "Ottawa is Canada's best kept secret...even if it is the coldest major capital in the world."

Toronto, Ontario's capital, with a population of 2,850,000, isn't a secret – not any more. From Toronto, bankers, businessmen and manufacturers run the nation's commerce. The city's commercial network has expanded along the curving western shoreline of Lake Ontario, from Oshawa to St. Catharines. Now called the Golden Horseshoe, this crescent has become Canada's only megalopolis, with 3.8 million people. Sleek skyscrapers clasp the horizon, including four of Canada's eleven chartered banks and hundreds of Canadian, foreign and multinational corporations. Beneath the towering edifices are miles of manufacturing plants. Forty-three percent of all the taxes paid in Canada come from the Golden Horseshoe, where wages exceed those in the U.S.

Toronto is the headquarters of the English-speaking press and the Provincial Government which presides over Ontario's clean, relatively crime-free cities. The province's 37 universities and colleges, its social services and superior health care, have worked like a magnet for outsiders. The mecca for immigrants has attracted as many as 260,000 non-English speaking peoples. That number excludes the half a million Franco-Ontarians, most of whom are bilingual. In the last decade outsiders have flooded in at a rate of 15,000 to 20,000 a year. Unlike New York City, where a similar migration occurred a half century ago and where minorities for the most part blend together, in Toronto the 71 ethnic groups live in urban enclaves. As an example, one radio station broadcasts in 30 languages, including Hindustani.

Until the 1940s Toronto, taking a back seat to Montreal, was a sort of nice but frumpy town. Then a happy set of circumstances began to unfold. The St. Lawrence Seaway opened the city's Lake Ontario port to ocean commerce. Newly discovered nickel, silver, and uranium deposits to the north embarked an economic upsurge. And money poured in from across the border. With a third of Canada's buying power and a fourth of its population collected within a hundred mile radius, Toronto became the nation's new financial and industrial center.

A conspicuous symbol of Toronto's growth is a $40-million tower – 1,815 feet, 5 inches tall. The Canadian National Tower (CN) is the loftiest free-standing structure in the world. Toronto's palate for cultural offerings has grown, too. Revered but insolvent, the Royal Alexander Theatre was facing destruction when discount store entrepreneur "Honest Ed" Mirvish bought it and restored its fading elegance. Now it is the place for international entertainers to display their talents. Galleries, museums, markets, concerts, theaters, shops, marvelous restaurants all add to Toronto's cosmopolitan flavor. Toronto is a summer tourist's paradise. However, temperatures drop to some uncivil degrees in the winter and more Canadians head to the Southern United States than vice versa. One loyal, but occasionally cold, Toronto resident suggested that the United States and Canadian boundaries should have been set vertically instead of horizontally. Nevertheless one of the dividing lines is a dynamic segment of water. It seems that all the greater snow geese in the world must be here, for fifty miles or more along the St. Lawrence River. It is fall, and when the last one has flown in from the Eastern Arctic, they number two hundred thousand. By the time the geese have gone, the waterway is unnegotiable except along its downstream stretch, where salt has intervened from the sea.

From the source of the St. Louis River, which begins in Minnesota and flows into Lake Superior, the St. Lawrence River measures about 1,900 miles. It drains close to 291,000 square miles of land, nearly six times the size of England. Coming out of Lake Ontario, this river journeys 750 miles to the sea. The Thousand Islands, actually nearer to 2,000, mark its beginning. Some of the islands are tiny granite outcrops, others are over a hundred acres. Barons of finance and industry once owned plush summer places on some of the more inhabitable islands. George Boldt, then manager of the Waldorf Hotel in New York City, commissioned a castle to be built on an island called Heart. Unfortunately his wife died and the castle remained unfinished. Some might consider the Thousand Islands greatest claim to fame, however, lies in having their name on a salad dressing!

The river weaves through the islands, overlapping the United States and Canadian boundary for about a hundred miles. It meets the U.S. locks of the St. Lawrence Seaway shortly before coming to Montreal. The St. Lawrence is predominantly a Canadian river. Though it encounters New York and Ontario, it is engulfed by Quebec. The river passes the great island city of Montreal, then Quebec City, finally pushing past the Gaspé Peninsula before pouring into the gulf.

The St. Lawrence River was discovered by Jacques Cartier in 1535. He named it after the day's patron saint then sailed up to the "island with a mountain" (Mont

Real). His progression towards China was intercepted by rapids which he named La Chine. About 1705 the Canadians built a one-and-a-half-foot-deep canal at Lachine – just deep enough for a canoe. Several more canals were constructed along the St. Lawrence River, but large, sea-going ships were still obstructed. Then, in the 1950s, President Dwight D. Eisenhower and Queen Elizabeth II officially dedicated the new St. Lawrence Seaway, allowing passage of vessels up to 730 feet long, 76 feet wide and drawing 26 feet.

The locks were built just large enough to accommodate the "lakers" – boats specifically designed for navigation on the Great Lakes. The length of the season still limits the amount of tonnage which can be transported yearly. The Seaway is closed from around mid-December to early April. Advocates for extending the season to eleven months argue that icebreakers can cut through ice as thick as three feet and they can push it around, keeping it loose. On top of that, experiments have shown that the ice usually knits smoothly back together after the booms have been opened for the passage of a vessel. Environmentalists, on the other hand, claim that winter ship traffic would have damaging effects on ecology, fishery resources and wildlife habitats along the St. Lawrence. Both factions have a case.

Many days downstream from the Thousand Islands is a point where the St. Lawrence takes the flow of the Saguenay River. From that intersection one can take a ferry to Tadoussac, a town from the late 1500s. The one-time seasonal trading post became the best place on the St. Lawrence for whale-watching. Belugas – small white whales – are lured to the mouth of the Saguenay by rich marine life. Unfortunately, over-hunting has thinned the once-abundant supply of whales in the St. Lawrence. To make matters worse, in the 1930s the government of Quebec Province put a bounty on belugas to pacify fishermen, who blamed the mammals for the decline in their catches of cod and other fish. At the Île aux Coudres, west of Tadoussac, belugas were once trapped in a maze of saplings. That has stopped, but a whale sighting today is quite rare.

Farther downstream in Trois-Rivières, one of the three paper mills employs more than a thousand persons to produce 1,050 tons of newsprint daily. Nearby, another plant produces close to 450,000 tons a year. About 75 per cent of the paper used to print the New York Daily News comes from there. In addition, shipments are sent to many parts of the world, including China.

From Lake Ontario to Quebec City, the St. Lawrence has a quiet demeanor, maintaining a regularity of flow. From there to its mouth – where the ocean at high tide pours in more than 12 times the amount of water that flows out at low tide – the St. Lawrence assumes a different personality. It becomes a roiling river and its depth reaches more than a thousand feet in places.

Quebec City, framed with ancient, fortress-like walls, views the St. Lawrence from a lofty perch. Its narrow, cobblestone streets, antiquated buildings and spired churches add to its Old World charm.

Montreal, Quebec's most regal city, sits on a foot-shaped island thirty miles long and less than ten miles wide. In the middle of it is a mountain called Royal. Three million people live in Montreal, the second largest port in Canada, where vessels from sixty countries call. Great liners of the world used to dock there too, carrying as many as 200,000 passengers a year, but today only two passenger lines continue to use the port. Montreal's importance to the Canadian economy has increased since the St. Lawrence has been kept open to the sea year around. Because of that winter navigation Montreal has pumped more than $300 million into the national economy. Montreal's six oil firms do their share to aid Canada's pocketbook, too. Fina, Shell, Imperial, and Texaco process more than 500,000 barrels of crude oil there each day. The Canadian Coast Guard services most of the 2,300 buoys between Montreal and the Gulf of St. Lawrence, and operates more than two dozen lighthouses along the river. Like the Great Lakes, the St. Lawrence has a history of disasters. There have been an estimated 10,000 wrecks on the river. At least four vessels went down with cargoes of gold and silver worth between $600,000 and $1,000,000 each. The St. Lawrence River is only one watery link to the Great Lakes.

Beyond the five giant bodies of water tens of thousands of smaller lakes weave throughout the States and Canada. Michigan, for example, has over eleven thousand small lakes, Minnesota has about fourteen thousand, and it is estimated that Ontario has thirty-five thousand just north of Superior, and a quarter of a million lakes in the entire Province. Those watery reservoirs are the Great Lakes region's playgrounds.

Fishing is the favored water sport and it is the most democratic. Anyone can fish. Fishermen who go after pan fish can simply dangle a line with a hook and a worm over the end of a dock or at the edge of the water; others fly-cast for trout in streams. A favorite catch is the walleye or northern pike and many a seasoned fisherman will settle for nothing less than a thirty-five-pound muskellunge (muskie). Finally, a group will take a fancy yacht or any available vessel to search for salmon in one of the Great Lakes. Even the casual sportsman feels a thrill when he pulls in one of the 240 species which swim in the region's lakes.

On summer weekends the Great Lakes and its tributaries burgeon with boats. The Sunday flotilla of pontoons, inboard and outboard motor boats, cabin cruisers and sailing craft express a subculture which souls bound to shore will never know. Almost half the numbered pleasure boats in the United States are registered in the eight Great Lakes States. Water-skiing behind power boats has become an organized sport. Fifty-three regional water-ski clubs support regular tournaments with such events as slalom skiing, three-story pyramids, barefoot skiing, and, more recently, kite-flying, a type of hang-gliding. The kite is generally a colorful delta wing measuring about thirteen feet six inches, with which the skier soars two to three hundred feet, although some brave kite-flyers have gone as high as fourteen hundred feet. Spectators participate vicariously as they watch the kaleidoscope of color sail toward the sky.

Cruising the Great Lakes can be an adventuresome pastime because of their accessibility to faraway places. From Detroit, for instance, a cruiser can cross Lakes Erie and Ontario to Kingston, journey up the Rideau Canal to Ottawa, and dock within a block of Parliament Hill.

From Ottawa, a cruiser can travel down the Ottawa River to Montreal, go east or west on the St. Lawrence or down the Richelieu Canal system to Lake Champlain. It can work its way down the Hudson to New York City and up the Hudson again to Albany. From there it can move west across New York State, enter Lake Erie near Buffalo and cruise all the way to Lake Superior.

An alternative route from Detroit would be to follow the Lakes around Michigan's Lower Peninsula, going north and then south to Chicago. From there a boat can navigate to the Gulf of Mexico via the Illinois and Mississippi rivers.

Cruisers can reach Georgian Bay from any starting point along the Great Lakes. The giant body of water off Lake Huron is entered between the tip of Bruce Peninsula and Manitoulin Island. Ten thousand rocky islands lace the bay, making it a tourist's paradise.

From Port Severn on Georgian Bay, the cruiser can travel all the way to Port Wellington on eastern Lake Ontario. It would maneuver through Canadian locks and lakes on the Trent-Severn Waterway – a linkage of rivers, lakes and canals.

Yachtsmen who head for Lake Superior, journey through the Soo Canal at St. Mary's River. From Grand Portage on Lake Superior the Pigeon River leads to a realm of hundreds of lakes stretching to Alaska. The nearly limitless options from Great Lakes harbors could offer the cruise enthusiast a lifetime of pleasure and adventure.

Residents of Great Lakes country don't stay inside when those watery playgrounds freeze. People on either side of the border simply don more clothing and race outside to test their mettle at sports, plunging into more than 20 inches of snow and below zero temperatures. Both nations have skate fever. At Gilbert, Minnesota, 6 to 8-year-old "ice mice" learn how to send a hockey puck into the net. Eveleth, a nearby town of 5,000, has already sent 13 players to the National Hockey League; four of them are honored in Eveleth's newly-opened United States Hockey Hall of Fame. In Toronto, subways and sidewalks bristle with hockey sticks as thousands of youngsters prepare to play their way toward the professional ranks. The Toronto Maple Leafs are idols for the young participants in Canada's national sport.

Recreational skating plays a big part in the lives of lakeside residents too. Ponds, streams and lakes are transformed into ice rinks. As many as 35,000 Sunday skaters glide on a frozen six miles of the Rideau Canal.

Dog teams, once vital for winter transport, have given way to the snowmobile, developed by Minnesotans. Racers compete in an "International 500" on a course between Winnepeg, Manitoba, and St. Paul, Minnesota. Offering $39,000 in prize money, the contest is sponsored by St. Paul's Winter Carnival. Cross-country skiers think the snowmobile a despoiler of peace, however.

Downhill skiing has become the rage around the Great Lakes. Though no mountains surround them there are challenging slopes nearby. Swiss-looking chalets mark areas that were once reserved for wildlife. Although skiing is possible almost anywhere there is a snow-covered bump, skiers prefer more elevation. Those prominent hills are found in northern Wisconsin, the Upper Peninsula of Michigan and near Lake Superior's north shore at Lutsen, Minnesota and Thunder Bay, Ontario. Michigan's Lower Peninsula probably has the largest number of ski tows. Upper New York State and the Laurentians above Montreal can be crowded with skiers too. But the heaviest concentration of slopes cluster around Georgian Bay.

Each season heralds its particular sports. Fall is the harbinger of hunting. When the leaves change color, potential sharp-shooters begin to scrutinize both sky and land for evidence of their fine-feathered victims. A previously-ignored marsh becomes likely territory for a mallard or wood duck and a farmer's corn field is transformed into a haven for pheasants. Thousands of United States citizens flock across the border in quest of Canada's geese while others stay back home and intercept them on their way to warmer weather.

For those who prefer traveling a nature trail to sitting in a duck blind, the Great Lakes region offers over 675 state parks. Hikers, campers and backpackers can find paths which have scarcely been touched since the Indians used them. Even the most popular paths have not suffered from overcrowding. The well-known Bruce Trail, some 433 miles long, goes from Niagara Falls to the very tip of Bruce Peninsula at Tobermory. There are many less grand pathways, but the maverick who rejects formally-designated trails can wander through thousands of acres of national, state and provincial parks, forests and wilderness areas.

The Great Lakes are a precious national resource, providing subsistence and pleasure to millions of people from two nations. Can we continue to abuse them? What greater legacy could we leave our children than five clean inland seas?

Previous page: a pleasure boat passes one of the islands in St. Lawrence Islands National Park. These pages: the United States' bridge, between Wellesley Island and the south bank of the river. The Thousand Islands International Bridge (overleaf) links with the bridge from Wellesley Island, leading to the Thousand Islands Skydeck on Hill Island.

Above: the City Hall of Kingston, Ontario, which was begun in the 1840s when the town temporarily became the capital of the Province of Canada. **Facing page:** the castle built in the 1890s by millionaire George Boldt for his wife. When she died he abandoned the heart-shaped island for ever. **Overleaf:** Rochester, New York State, (left) Windsor Beach and (right) the U.S. Coastguard station.

These pages: the fine architecture of the University of Rochester, situated in the third
largest city in New York State. Overleaf: (left) a marina at Olcott, near the eastern end
of Lake Ontario, and (right) Braddock Bay State Marina at Manitou Beach, near Rochester.

Above: the shore of Lake Ontario in Wilson Tuscarora State Park and (facing page) the marina at nearby Olcott, both in New York State.

These pages and overleaf: Toronto is the largest city in Canada and bustles with life and excitement. Above: sunset over Lake Ontario, (facing page and overleaf, left) Ontario Place, and (overleaf, right) a steamer passing Toronto Islands.

Previous pages: (left) Ontario Place and the Exhibition Grounds and (right) a popular beach on Toronto Islands. These pages: the Ice Canoe Race across Toronto Harbour, held as part of the Molson Winterfest. Overleaf: the towering pinnacle of the CN Tower, which dominates the skyline of Toronto.

Previous pages: two spectacular views of the lip of Niagara Falls. Above: the bitter cold of winter can cause the turbulent waters beneath the falls to ice over, and even the falls themselves are bedecked with snow and ice. Facing page and overleaf: the *Maid of the Mist* boats take visitors into the heart of the spray to view the grandeur of the falls from below.

Previous pages: (left) the water disappearing over Niagara Falls and (right) the turbulent river upstream of the falls. Buffalo (these pages and overleaf) may stand in New York State, but there can be little doubt that its heart lies in the Mid-west. It is a town of the Great Lakes, with far more in common with Chicago than with New York City.

These pages and overleaf: Buffalo, the New York State city on the shores of Lake Erie. Facing page and overleaf, right: the distinctive City Hall, an Art Deco extravaganza of 1932. Overleaf: (left) the War Memorial and (right) the McKinley Monument in front of City Hall, commemorating President McKinley who was shot in Buffalo in 1901.

ge: the solid, stone structure of Erie County Hall in
Above: sunset gilds the sky above the Erie Marina. Overleaf:
Marina, in the heart of Buffalo, during the heat of the day.

Previous pages: contrasting views of the Coastguard Lighthouse at the Erie Basin Marina, Buffalo. Left: State Street, Erie. Bottom left: boy fishing and (bottom right and below) the beach at Presque Isle. Facing page: sunset over Lake Erie in Pennsylvania. Overleaf: (left) fountains outside the Cleveland Convention Center and (right) the 708-foot-high Terminal Tower in downtown Cleveland.

Previous pages: (left) the mouth of the Rocky River and (right) Edgewater Park, both on Lake Erie near Cleveland. Above: lakeshore houses and (facing page) a marina, both in Vermilion, west of Cleveland. Overleaf: (left) Cedar Point, Sandusky, has dozens of rides and a huge marina and is considered the finest entertainment center on the lakes, and (right) Toledo.

pages: (left) the southernmost point of Canada, in Point Pelee National Park, and (right) nearby frozen by the winter cold. Facing page: Detroit's Jefferson Avenue. Above and overleaf, left: the Ambassador Bridge over the Detroit River. Overleaf, right: Detroit from Windsor, Ontario.

The automobile has left an indelible mark on the face of heavily-industrialized Detroit (these pages and overleaf). More recently, however, the city has made strenuous efforts to change its image by entering the world of art and culture. Facing page and overleaf, left: the Renaissance Center, one of Detroit's more impressive buildings. Overleaf, right: the Dodge Fountain.

Georgian Bay Islands National Park was set up by the Canadian
Government to preserve the beauty captured by the "Group of
Seven" artists. It is one of the smallest parks in the system,
covering only 13.8 square kilometres scattered among 50 islands.
Facing page: the quiet, leaf-covered trail through the woods
near Castle Bluff, Flowerpot Island. Above: a scene at Finger
Point.

Facing page: the sun filters through the overhanging branches and foliage to create a lovely woodland scene on Beausoliel Island, the largest in Georgian Bay Islands National Park. Top left: the view from Castle Bluff along the north shore of Flowerpot Island. Above Castle Bluff are the caves and rock formations (top right). Left: "Large Flowerpot" on Flowerpot Island, where the bunchberry (above) and the one-leaf rein orchis (top center) are also found.

Above: the graceful sweep of the five-mile-long Straits of Mackinac Bridge which connects the two peninsulas of Michigan. Facing page and overleaf, left: views across Mackinac Island, where automobiles are banned, from Fort Mackinac. Overleaf, right: Fort Michilimackinac is a restoration on the original foundations of the fort built in 1715 by the French. The strongpoint subsequently passed to the British, in 1761, who promptly lost it to the Chippewa Indians during Pontiac's Uprising. It was recaptured in 1764 and finally abandoned in 1781, when the garrison moved to Mackinac Island.

Previous pages: (left) Upper Herring Lake, near Frankfort and (right) evening on Traverse Bay on Lake Michigan. Above: the Old School House on the Lee Lanau Peninsula. Facing page: the Old Mission Lighthouse, with an explanatory sign. Overleaf: (left) Sleeping Bear Dunes National Lakeshore near Frankfort and (right) the lighthouse at nearby Point Betsie.

The seven million people who live in Chicago make this the second largest city in the nation and one of the most dynamic. Above: the Gothic-style Tribune Tower and the Wrigley Building, clad in white terracotta, on the "Magnificent Mile". Facing page: the black mass of the John Hancock Tower dominates the city. Overleaf: the glittering night-time skyline of Chicago.

Previous pages: (left) the gleaming glass face of 333 Wacker Drive and (right) West Lake Street underneath The Loop. These pages: two of the many marinas which serve Chicago's boating enthusiasts. Overleaf: (left) the gleaming Wrigley Building and Gothic Tribune Tower and (right) the distinctive, white "Big Stan" skyscraper.

Milwaukee (these pages and overleaf) is the center of Wisconsin's trade network, but is probably better known as the brewing capital of the nation. These pages: ducks stand on the frozen waters of Lakeside Park. Overleaf: (bottom left) Wisconsin Avenue, (bottom center and top center) Peck Pavilion and the Performing Arts Center and (right) the Milwaukee River.

Previous pages: (left) Fayette State Park, a ghost industrial town on the Upper Peninsula, and (right) the grimly-named Death's Door in Wisconsin. One of mankind's greatest engineering projects reaches its end at Sault Ste. Marie (these pages and overleaf). At these locks, between Lakes Huron and Superior, ships travelling the St. Lawrence Seaway are raised the final few feet on their journey.

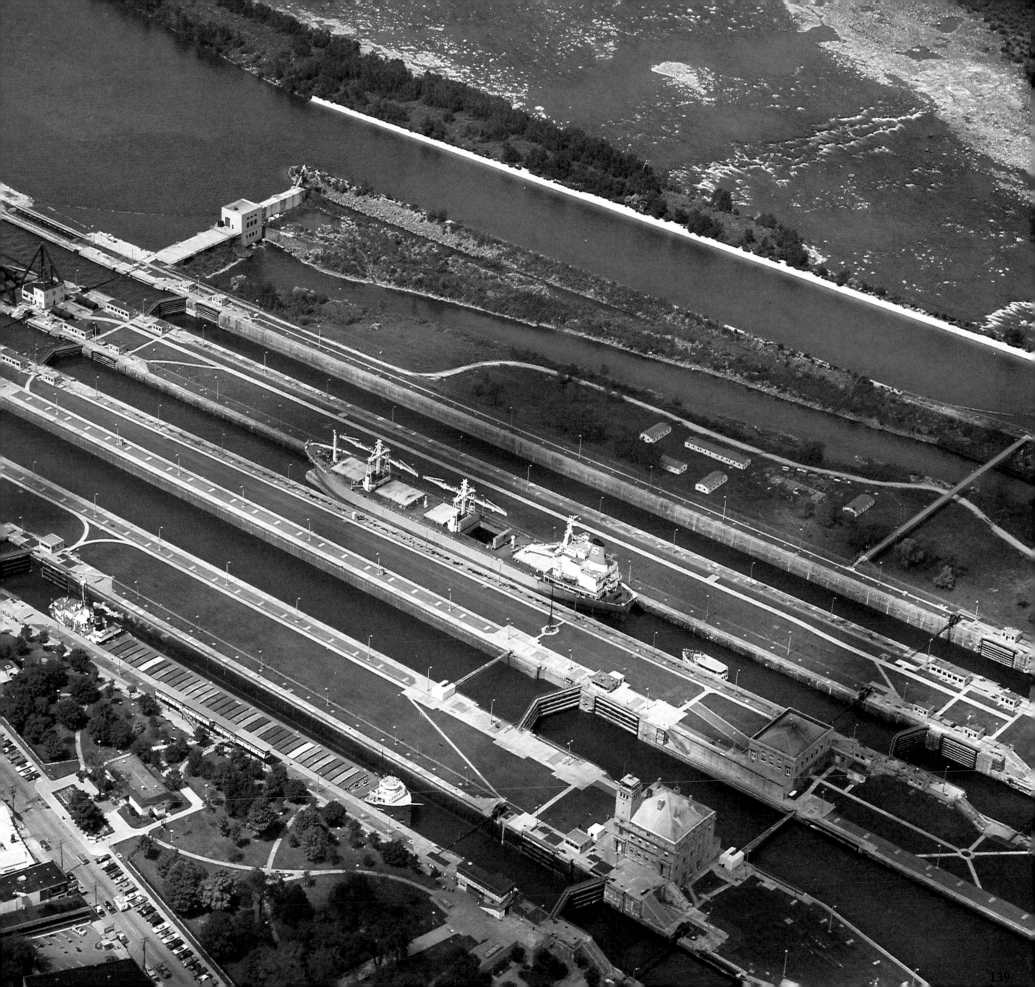

Seen from the Tower of History, Sault Ste. Marie (above) stretches away towards the International Bridge into Canada. This small town claims to be the third oldest settlement in the United States. Facing page: the town's SS Valley Camp Museum. Overleaf: (left) sunset near the Point Iriqui Lighthouse (right), just one of the many signals on the lakes.

These pages: the tannic-acid-stained waters of the Lower Tahquamenon Falls tumble through Michigan's Upper Peninsula. Overleaf: the 48-foot drop of the Upper Tahquamenon Falls churns the soft water of the river into a welter of foam which has made the Tahquamenon River famous since its earliest exploration.

The Pictured Rocks, immortalized in Longfellow's poem *Hiawatha*, were designated a National Lakeshore in 1966 and lie some 5 miles northeast of Munising. The spectacular formations are generally best seen from the surface of Lake Superior, but Miner's Castle (facing page) can be appreciated from land. Above: nearby Munising waterfall. Overleaf: (left) an old copper mine at Houghton and (right) the Eagle Harbor Lighthouse, both on the Keweenaw Peninsula.

Above: a golden sunset at Presque Isle Point on Lake Superior, near Marquette on the Upper Peninsula. Facing page: the steel structure of the Houghton Hancock Bridge, whose central section lifts to allow ships to pass through. Overleaf, left: the restored frontier fortress of Fort Wilkins. Now at the center of a 199-acre State Park, Fort Wilkins was established in 1844 and held until it was abandoned in 1870. Three miles west of the fort is Copper Harbor (overleaf, right) on the Keweenaw Peninsula, from which many pleasure boats put out onto Lake Superior.

These pages: the pale rays of evening sunlight spread across the winter snows at
Port Wing, on Wisconsin's Lake Superior shoreline. Overleaf: frozen marshes and
driftwood on the shores of Lake Superior near Port Wing.

Duluth marks the farthest west that any ship can travel via the St. Lawrence Seaway from the Atlantic some 2,300 miles distant. Previous pages: (left) the lift bridge which spans the ship canal at the entrance to the harbor and (right) a Coast Guard boat. Above: Duluth Harbor. Facing page: the expanse of Lake Superior beyond the harbor. Overleaf: pleasure boats in the harbor.

pages: the peaceful shores of Lake Superior from Hartman Park. These pages: evening sunlight on the
ard Station and lighthouse at Grand Marais on Lake Superior. Overleaf: (left) Two Harbors, which lies
long the north shore of the lake and (right) the rocky shore near the mouth of the Baptism River.

Above: harebells on the rocky shore at Grand Marais. Facing page: the Ash River in Voyageurs National Park. Overleaf: (left) lichens, overlooking Lake Superior near the mouth of the Baptism River and (right) sunset over the lake at Grand Marais.

of Thunder Bay (above) was formed in 1970 when the two towns of Port Arthur and Fort William amalgamated and
r name from the stretch of water (facing page) by which they stand. The rail lines which snake into the port
west bring millions of bushels of grain to be stored in the massive grain elevators (overleaf, left) prior to
ment. Overleaf, right: the Great Lakes Paper Mill and Mount Mackay.

179

Previous pages, left, these pages and overleaf: the Canadian Ski Jumping
Championships at Thunder Bay. Previous pages, right: the Great Lakes Paper Mill,
whose massive output contributes to the prosperity of Thunder Bay.

"Superior is a sea: she breeds storms and rain and fog like the sea... She is wild, masterful and dreaded."
The truth of the Reverend George Grant's words is all too apparent when viewing the rocky coast (above) and
the storm-tossed debris hurled on the shore (facing page), both in Pukaskwa National Park, Ontario. Overleaf:
(left) a typical farm near Thunder Bay and (right) sunset over Millbay.

188